# Project Management Fundamentals (Third Edition)

# Project Management Fundamentals (Third Edition)

Part Number: 095015
Course Edition: 1.1

## Acknowledgements

### PROJECT TEAM

| Author | Media Designer | Content Editor |
| --- | --- | --- |
| Sunni K Brock | Brian Sullivan | Peter Bauer |

Logical Operations wishes to thank the Logical Operations Instructor Community, and in particular John Wilson, for their instructional and technical expertise during the creation of this course.

## Notices

# Project Management Fundamentals (Third Edition)


**Lesson 1: Getting Started with Project Management........ 1**

Topic A: Identify the Characteristics of a Project........................... 2

Topic B: Identify the Project Management Life Cycle..................... 5

Topic C: Identify the Role of a Project Manager............................ 10

**Lesson 2: Initiating a Project..................................... 17**

Topic A: Determine the Scope of a Project................................... 18

Topic B: Identify the Skills for a Project Team.............................. 24

Topic C: Identify the Risks to a Project........................................ 29

**Lesson 3: Planning for Time and Cost.......................... 35**

Topic A: Create a WBS................................................................ 36

Topic B: Sequence the Activities................................................. 39

Topic C: Create a Project Schedule.............................................. 43

Topic D: Determine Project Costs................................................ 49

**Lesson 4: Planning for Project Risks, Communication, and Change Control................................................ 53**

Topic A: Analyze the Risks to a Project.................................................. 54

Topic B: Create a Communication Plan................................................ 57

Topic C: Plan for Change Control........................................................60


**Lesson 5: Managing a Project................................................. 65**

Topic A: Begin Project Work................................................................66

Topic B: Execute the Project Plan........................................................ 69

Topic C: Track Project Progress........................................................... 72

Topic D: Report Performance............................................................... 77

Topic E: Implement Change Control..................................................... 80


**Lesson 6: Closing the Project.................................................83**

Topic A: Close a Project......................................................................84

Topic B: Create a Final Report.............................................................86


**Appendix A: Logical Operations Master Mobile Application Developer
(MMAD) Exam MAD-111 Objectives............................................... 93**

**Solutions................................................................................ 105**

**Glossary................................................................................. 117**

**Index..................................................................................... 121**

# About This Course

Successfully managing a project requires effective planning and adherence to the industry's best practices in every step of the process. By understanding the fundamentals of project management, you will be better prepared to initiate a project in your organization and position it for success. In this course, you will identify effective project management practices and their related processes.

At this point in your professional development, you are ready to take on the responsibility for managing projects. You can manage a project by developing a solid understanding of the fundamentals of project management and its underlying structure and elements, including project phases, project life cycles, stakeholders, and areas of expertise. These, coupled with the ability to identify the project management processes that are recognized industry-wide as good practice, will help you to apply effective project management techniques to improve the efficiency of your projects and ensure their success.

This course is also designed to assist candidates who are preparing for the Master Mobile Application Developer (MMAD) (Exam MAD-111) certification examination. What you learn and practice in this course can be a significant part of your preparation for the project management portions of that certification.

## Course Description

### Target Student

This course is designed for individuals whose primary job is not project management, but who manage projects on an informal basis. Also, anyone who is considering a career path in project management and desiring a complete overview of the field and its generally accepted practices can benefit from this course.

### Course Prerequisites

To ensure your success, you will need to take the following Logical Operations courses or have equivalent knowledge:

- *Microsoft® Office Word 2016: Part 1*

Some on-the-job experience in participating in managed projects would be preferable.

### Course Objectives

In this course, you will examine the elements of sound project management and apply the generally recognized practices to successfully manage projects.

You will:

- Identify the key processes and requirements of project management.
- Initiate a project.

- Plan for time and cost.
- Plan for project risks, communication, and change control.
- Execute, manage, and control a project.
- Close a project.

## The CHOICE Home Screen

Logon and access information for your CHOICE environment will be provided with your class experience. The CHOICE platform is your entry point to the CHOICE learning experience, of which this course manual is only one part.

On the CHOICE Home screen, you can access the CHOICE Course screens for your specific courses. Visit the CHOICE Course screen both during and after class to make use of the world of support and instructional resources that make up the CHOICE experience.

Each CHOICE Course screen will give you access to the following resources:

- **Classroom**: A link to your training provider's classroom environment.
- **eBook**: An interactive electronic version of the printed book for your course.
- **Files**: Any course files available to download.
- **Checklists**: Step-by-step procedures and general guidelines you can use as a reference during and after class.
- **LearnTOs**: Brief animated videos that enhance and extend the classroom learning experience.
- **Assessment**: A course assessment for your self-assessment of the course content.
- Social media resources that enable you to collaborate with others in the learning community using professional communications sites such as LinkedIn or microblogging tools such as Twitter.

Depending on the nature of your course and the components chosen by your learning provider, the CHOICE Course screen may also include access to elements such as:

- LogicalLABS, a virtual technical environment for your course.
- Various partner resources related to the courseware.
- Related certifications or credentials.
- A link to your training provider's website.
- Notices from the CHOICE administrator.
- Newsletters and other communications from your learning provider.
- Mentoring services.

Visit your CHOICE Home screen often to connect, communicate, and extend your learning experience!

## How to Use This Book

### As You Learn

This book is divided into lessons and topics, covering a subject or a set of related subjects. In most cases, lessons are arranged in order of increasing proficiency.

The results-oriented topics include relevant and supporting information you need to master the content. Each topic has various types of activities designed to enable you to solidify your understanding of the informational material presented in the course. Information is provided for reference and reflection to facilitate understanding and practice.

Data files for various activities as well as other supporting files for the course are available by download from the CHOICE Course screen. In addition to sample data for the course exercises, the course files may contain media components to enhance your learning and additional reference materials for use both during and after the course.

Checklists of procedures and guidelines can be used during class and as after-class references when you're back on the job and need to refresh your understanding.

At the back of the book, you will find a glossary of the definitions of the terms and concepts used throughout the course. You will also find an index to assist in locating information within the instructional components of the book.

## As You Review

Any method of instruction is only as effective as the time and effort you, the student, are willing to invest in it. In addition, some of the information that you learn in class may not be important to you immediately, but it may become important later. For this reason, we encourage you to spend some time reviewing the content of the course after your time in the classroom.

## As a Reference

The organization and layout of this book make it an easy-to-use resource for future reference. Taking advantage of the glossary, index, and table of contents, you can use this book as a first source of definitions, background information, and summaries.

## Course Icons

Watch throughout the material for the following visual cues.

| Icon | Description |
| --- | --- |
| | A **Note** provides additional information, guidance, or hints about a topic or task. |
| | A **Caution** note makes you aware of places where you need to be particularly careful with your actions, settings, or decisions so that you can be sure to get the desired results of an activity or task. |
| | **LearnTO** notes show you where an associated LearnTO is particularly relevant to the content. Access LearnTOs from your CHOICE Course screen. |
| | **Checklists** provide job aids you can use after class as a reference to perform skills back on the job. Access checklists from your CHOICE Course screen. |
| | **Social** notes remind you to check your CHOICE Course screen for opportunities to interact with the CHOICE community using social media. |

# 1 Getting Started with Project Management

**Lesson Time: 1 hour**

## Lesson Introduction

You actively participated in a project. Now, you want to move from participating in projects to managing projects. In this lesson, you will be introduced to the basic terminology used in project management, examine the phases in a project's life cycle, and identify the roles and responsibilities of a project manager.

To be a successful project manager, you need to be able to use your management skills with sound knowledge of the processes to achieve your goals. By identifying the key elements of effective project management practice, you can enhance your chances of success in managing a wide range of projects across application areas and industries.

## Lesson Objectives

In this lesson, you will:

- Identify the characteristics of a project.

- Identify the project management life cycle.

- Identify the role of a project manager.

# TOPIC A

# Identify the Characteristics of a Project

Before you begin to play a role in managing a project, you need to know everything about the project in detail. In this topic, you will define a project and identify its characteristics.

Business organizations around the world use project management as a competitive advantage to achieve corporate strategic objectives. Before beginning to apply the principles of project management on your job, you need to know what a project is and how it is different from other day-to-day activities.

## Projects

A *project* is a temporary endeavor that creates a unique product, service, or result. It has a clearly defined duration. It develops in steps and continues to grow in increments. The end of a project is reached when its objectives are met, or the need for the project no longer exists, or it is determined that the objectives cannot be met. Projects can vary widely in terms of budget, team size, duration, expected outcomes, and industries.

### Example: Project to Develop a Word Processor

Consider a project authorized by a software firm to develop a new version of a word processor. The outcome of the project is the word processor application. The duration of the project depends on the complexity and size of the work involved and the organization's business objectives. The project will come to an end when the product is ready for distribution in the market.

## Operational Tasks and Projects

Operational tasks are ongoing and repetitive tasks that produce the same outcome every time they are performed, whereas projects are temporary endeavors with a unique outcome. Whereas the purpose of operational tasks is to carry out day-to-day activities and sustain the business, the purpose of projects is to meet specific objectives. Projects conclude when their objectives are met, but operational tasks adopt new objectives and the work continues.

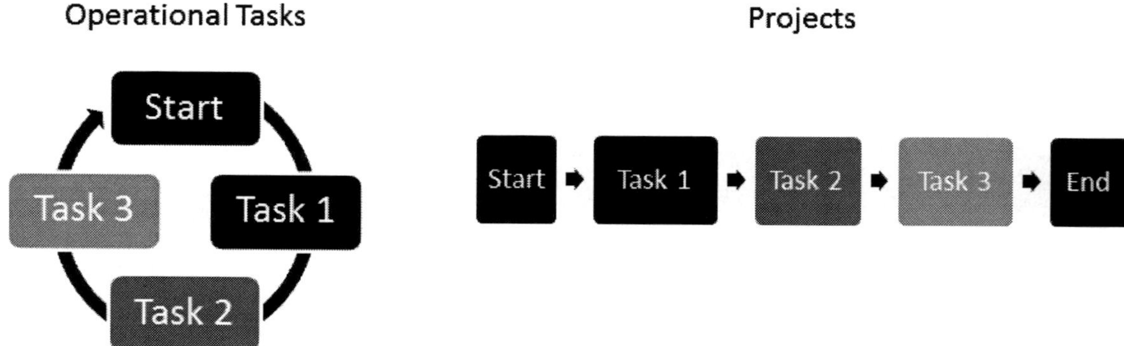


*Figure 1–1: Operational tasks repeat indefinitely; project have a definite start and end.*

## The Project Life Cycle

The *project life cycle* is the sequence of *project phases*, which break a project down into manageable, sequential phases of work activities to improve management control. Project life cycles may have four or five phases, which vary in the customized life cycle versions. The project life cycle is marked by the beginning and the end of the project. During the initial phase, the project's objectives and timing are determined. During the intermediate phases, detailed planning occurs along with the actual work activities. In the final phase, project-closing activities occur.

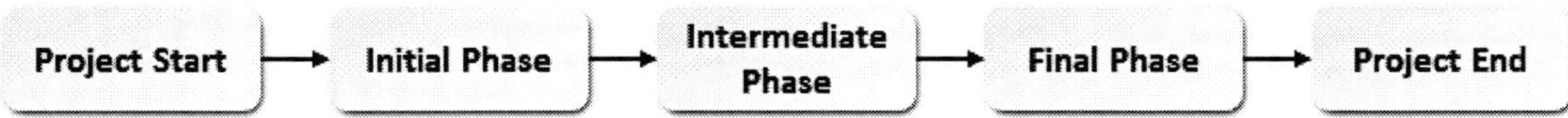

*Figure 1-2: The project life cycle is made up of the project phases.*

# Need for a Project

Projects serve as a means for carrying out activities that cannot be performed like the other operational tasks. They form a part of an organization's strategic plan and enable the organization to achieve the plan. An organization takes up a project based on strategic considerations, such as an organizational need, a market demand, a customer request, a technological advancement, or a legal requirement.

# Project Stakeholders

A *project stakeholder* is a person who has a business interest in the outcome of a project. Project stakeholders exert influence on the objectives of a project. Their expectations and needs have to be identified and met for a project to deliver a successful outcome. They have different responsibilities and command varying levels of authority over a project.

## Example: Project Stakeholders for a Construction Project

David Anderson is a project manager supervising the expansion of a large municipal public library. David identifies that the stakeholders in this project include government agencies, taxpayers, the voters who have voted to authorize the city to issue bonds for the project, and private donors who have contributed towards costs.

# Types of Project Stakeholders

A project can have different types of stakeholders.

| Project Stakeholder | Responsibility |
| --- | --- |
| Sponsor | An individual or group that provides financial resources for a project. |
| Customer | An individual or organization that will use the project's output and pays for it. |
| Project manager | An individual who is responsible for managing a project. |
| Project team | A group that performs the work on a project. |
| Project management team | The members of a project team who perform the project management activities. |

# ACTIVITY 1–1
## Identifying Project Basics

### Scenario

You are part of a group of tax return processors. Every day the group interviews clients, uses the data to fill out tax returns, and computes the amount of tax owed. Your coworker, Rita, manages a team that is developing a training manual to help new tax return processors learn their jobs faster. Her team is made up of tax return specialists, writers, and graphic designers who are assigned to the team part-time. The work must be completed by January 1 in time for Human Resources to train the new tax return processors who will be hired next year. Rita is going on vacation, and you've been asked by your manager, Bob, to manage the team during her absence. You need to start by identifying basic details about the project.

1. What are the characteristics of the project that Rita's team is working on that make it a project instead of an operational task?

2. Who are the stakeholders (project manager, customer, sponsor, project team, project management team) for the training manual project?

3. It is common for project teams to have part-time members who also perform operational tasks. Which team members also have operational tasks? What are the operational tasks? How might this impact the project?

# TOPIC B

# Identify the Project Management Life Cycle

You defined a project and identified its characteristics. Before assuming project management responsibilities, you need to identify how project management functions within an organization and how it serves to achieve the objectives of the business. In this topic, you will describe the project management life cycle.

To perform project management duties successfully, you need to get a clear idea of what project management is, identify how an organization aligns the ongoing projects with its strategic goals, and analyze how a project is managed. For this, you need to define project, program, and portfolio management, and describe the project management life cycle.

## Project Management

*Project management* is the management of project activities to meet the project's objectives. It is accomplished through the application and integration of knowledge, skills, tools, and techniques to project activities. It not only involves scheduling and getting the work done, but also includes identifying requirements; establishing objectives; balancing quality, scope, time, and cost; and addressing the concerns and expectations of the stakeholders. Project management may differ from project to project depending on the activities that need to be performed and the tools and techniques to be used.

### Example: Project Management Involved in Building a New Wind Farm

Project management is required to manage the activities involved in building a new wind farm authorized by an alternative energy company. The project manager must grapple with communicating cross-functionally, manage the efforts of people who are external or internal to the company, and deliver the work on time, within the allotted budget, and within the specifications for quality.

## Program

A *program* is a group of related projects that may have a common objective. It offers greater control over the constituent projects and delivers benefits that the organization can utilize to meet its goals. A program is generally managed by a program manager, and the individual projects are managed by project managers who work for the program manager. In some organizations, a program is viewed as ongoing work without a clear end point.

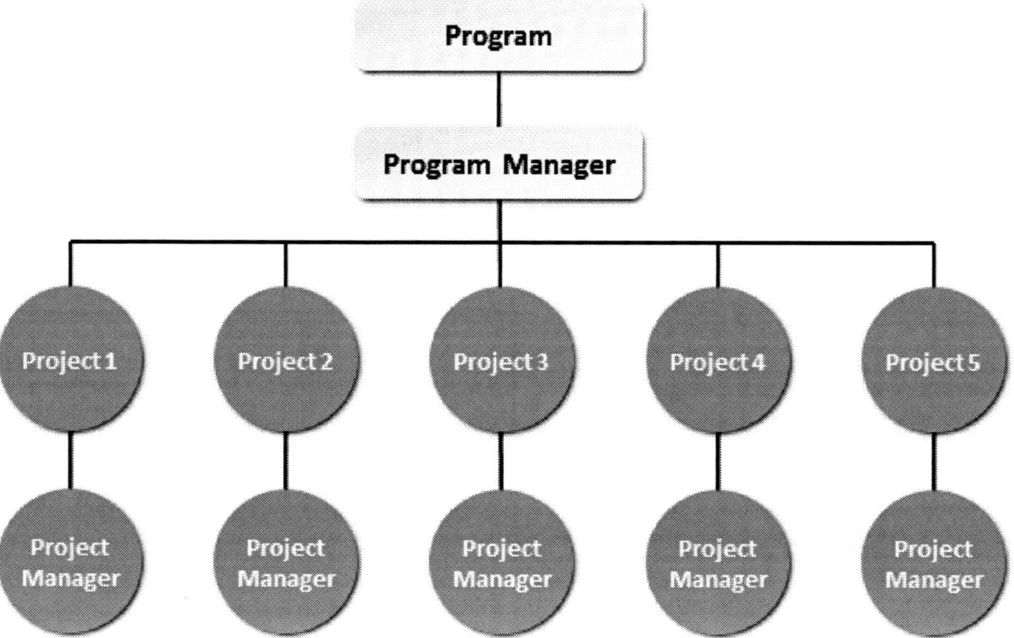


*Figure 1-3: A program encompasses multiple related projects.*

### Example: Program to Build a Residential Complex

Building with Heart, a residential construction organization, has proposed a new program that involves building a large residential complex, which will include a number of smaller projects.

## Program Management

*Program management* is the management of a program in a centralized and coordinated manner to achieve the program's objectives and benefits. It involves managing work that is beyond the scope of the individual projects in a program. Program management includes managing multiple discrete projects and integrating them towards a common goal. It requires managers to manage the interdependencies between the projects by allocating resources, prioritizing efforts, and maintaining the projects' alignment with business objectives.

### Example: The Apollo Program

The Apollo program's mission was to put a man on the moon within 10 years. Apollo 1, 2, and 3 were short-term projects within the Apollo program.

## Portfolio

A *portfolio* is a collection of programs or projects that are grouped to achieve an organization's strategic business objectives. The projects in a portfolio may or may not be interdependent, but they are grouped to give management a broader view of the organization's projects and their adherence to organizational objectives. For a project to be part of a portfolio, its attributes such as cost, requirement of resources, timelines, and benefits should be in line with the other projects in the portfolio and the strategic goals the portfolio is expected to meet. Portfolios are generally managed by a senior manager or senior management teams.

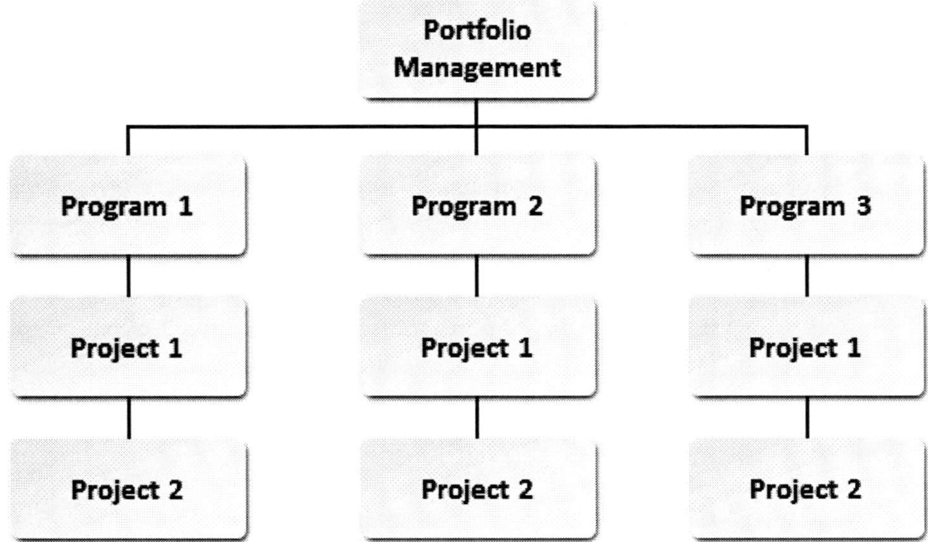


*Figure 1-4: A portfolio encompasses multiple programs and projects.*

## Example: Portfolio at an Energy Company

An energy company has started a portfolio that involves designing a breakthrough technology capitalizing on solar energy. This portfolio includes a number of smaller programs and projects; each of these smaller programs contains a series of projects.

# Portfolio Management

*Portfolio management* is the handling of a portfolio to ensure that all projects in the portfolio contribute to achieving the organization's strategic goals. It allows managers a global, top-down view of the health and viability of all the projects in the portfolio. Portfolio management strives to maximize the value of a portfolio by carefully selecting projects to be included in the portfolio and excluding those that are not meeting the strategic objectives. Portfolio management may be different in each organization as it depends on the organization's strategic objectives and business needs.

## Example: Portfolio Management at a Construction Company

The senior management of a construction company uses portfolio management to manage their residential, commercial, and infrastructure-based projects. Their goal is to gain ground on residential projects while ensuring that the projects meet strategic objectives set by the organization.

# Project Deliverable

A *project deliverable* is an output from a project management activity that is measurable, unique, and verifiable. Project deliverables require the approval and sign-off of the project stakeholders. The deliverables of one phase of a project serve as inputs to the subsequent phase. The project manager and the stakeholders determine the project deliverables based on the size and requirements of a project.

## Example: Project Deliverable of a Project at Develetech Industries

Develetech Industries, a home electronics company, has proposed a project for updating a mobile application with more features. The project deliverable of this project will be the final version of the updated software, the features of which will have to be approved by the customers, users, and other key stakeholders.

# Project Management Process Groups

Project management process groups are all the groups of activities that underlie the effective practice of project management. Many processes fall into each group. There are five formal process groups in the project management life cycle. They are:

1. **Initiating:** Defines a project and formally authorizes its start.
2. **Planning:** Defines project objectives and scope, and plans the steps to be taken to meet those objectives.
3. **Execution:** Organizes the project team and carries out the tasks required to complete the project.
4. **Monitoring and Controlling:** Surveys project execution to identify problems, take corrective action, and ensure that the project is on track.
5. **Closing:** Brings the project to a formal completion, irrespective of whether the objectives are met or not.

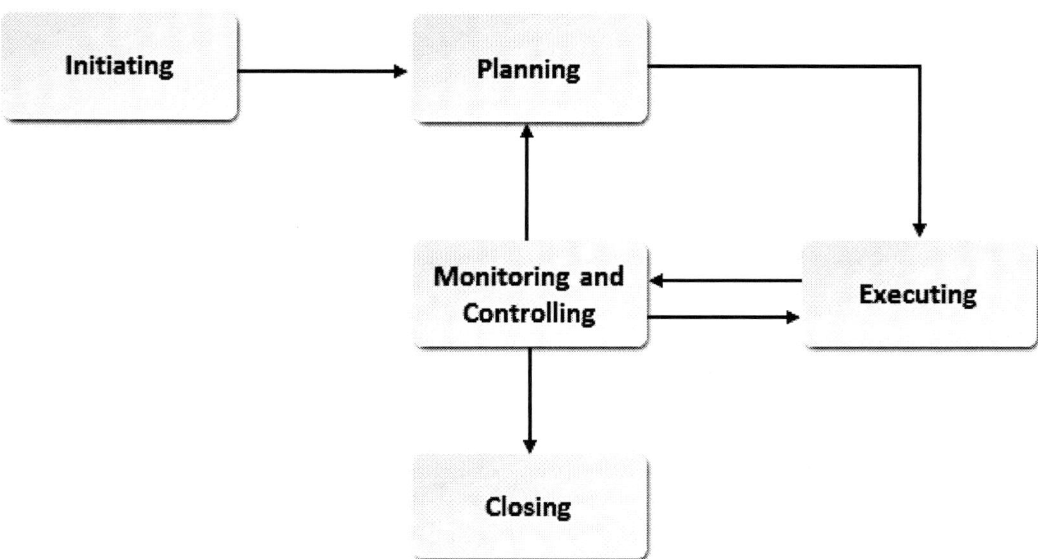


*Figure 1–5: The project management life cycle includes the five process groups.*

## Project Management vs. Product Development Standards

Product development standards and project management methodologies are sometimes confused with one another. Product development methodologies provide details for how work is to be performed to ensure product quality. For example, ISO 9001 requires that a design process includes such activities as requirements definition, planning, verification, and validation. Project management also includes requirements definition and planning, but project requirements and plans tend to be broader than those needed strictly for product development and are more likely to change during the course of the project.

# ACTIVITY 1–2
## Identifying the Project Management Life Cycle

## Scenario

Having taken over the project on developing the training manual from Rita, you need to identify the project management activities and processes required to start the project. You need to establish an understanding of how the project is to be managed, analyze the outcome of each process, and figure out the activities in which the stakeholders need to be involved.

1. **Which definition best describes project management?**
   - ○ Management of a collection of programs to ensure that all projects in the collection contribute to achieving the organization's strategic goals.
   - ○ Management of project activities to meet project objectives through the application of knowledge, skills, tools, and techniques to those activities.
   - ○ Management of a collection of projects in a centralized and coordinated manner to achieve collective objectives and benefits.
   - ○ Management of day-to-day activities to sustain the business.

2. **Give some examples of a portfolio and the programs and projects of which it is made up.**

3. **Which of these is the name of a project management process group?**
   - ○ Verification
   - ○ Prototyping
   - ○ Planning
   - ○ Designing

4. **True or False? A project deliverable requires the approval and sign-off of project stakeholders.**
   - ☐ True
   - ☐ False

5. **Which project management process group allows you to identify problems and take corrective action?**
   - ○ Monitoring and Controlling
   - ○ Execution
   - ○ Planning
   - ○ Initiation

6. **In which project management process group will you define a project's objectives and organize for the course of action to be taken?**
   - ○ Initiation
   - ○ Execution
   - ○ Monitoring and Controlling
   - ○ Planning

# TOPIC C

## Identify the Role of a Project Manager

Now that you know about projects and project management, you may be wondering about how to use it to attain your objectives. In this topic, you will identify the role of a project manager.

A project manager needs to coordinate the work of the team members and interact with people from different functions. To be successful in project management, you need to possess many skills other than traditional management and communication skills. Having a clear idea of the required skills will help you gain an insight into your role as a project manager.

## Skills of a Project Manager

Project managers need to possess multiple skills in order to be successful. They typically know a little about a number of areas and are very good communicators. They need to possess some leadership skills to motivate the team, and not only drive business decisions that may result in making trade-offs in the project, but also to get buy-in from stakeholders and sponsors by clearly articulating choices and recommendations. The skills of a project manager can be broadly classified into five categories.

| *Category* | *Description* |
| --- | --- |
| Project management knowledge | • Knowledge of project management tools and techniques.<br>• Ability to apply the project management knowledge to ongoing projects. |
| Knowledge of the application area | • Knowledge of the industry, functional departments, and technical elements.<br>• Familiarity with accepted standards and regulations. |
| Understanding of the project environment | • Understanding the impact of the project on the organization.<br>• Familiarity with the laws that could affect a project.<br>• Awareness of any physical impact a project may have on its physical environment. |
| General management knowledge and skills | • Ability to plan, organize, staff, execute, and control operations.<br>• Ability to manage time.<br>• Ability to estimate and budget.<br>• Ability to manage risks. |
| Interpersonal skills | • Ability to communicate with the senior management as well as the project team.<br>• Ability to influence decisions.<br>• Ability to lead a team.<br>• Ability to motivate.<br>• Ability to negotiate and manage conflicts.<br>• Ability to solve problems. |

# Types of Organizational Structures

The organizational structure determines how the individuals in an organization are grouped, how project teams are structured, and the level of authority the project manager has over the team. There are four types of organizational structures.

| Organizational Structure | Description |
| --- | --- |
| Functional | <ul><li>A hierarchical organization in which each employee reports to a functional manager.</li><li>Employees are grouped based on their area of expertise.</li><li>A project team may comprise members from different functions.</li><li>The authority of the project manager is lower compared to that of a functional manager.</li></ul> |
| Projectized | <ul><li>An organization having many organizational units called departments with individuals in each department reporting directly to a project manager.</li><li>Employees are grouped based on the projects they are working on.</li><li>The project manager has complete control and authority over the project team.</li></ul> |
| Matrix | <ul><li>An organization that follows a mix of the functional and projectized structures.</li><li>Individuals report directly to a functional manager but may also be controlled by a project manager.</li><li>A matrix structure can be characterized as strong, weak, or balanced based on the role of the project manager in the organization.</li><li>The authority of the project manager is greatest in a strong matrix structure and lowest in a weak matrix structure.</li></ul> |
| Composite | A combination of the functional, projectized, and matrix structures. An organization may choose to follow a different structure at different levels of the hierarchy. |

# Project Management Office

A *Project Management Office (PMO)* is an administrative unit that supervises and coordinates the management of all projects in an organization. The focus of a PMO is to achieve the organization's business objectives by prioritizing and directing the execution of projects. The PMO strives to improve the project management performance of the organization by identifying best practices and maintaining standards across projects. It also serves as a central repository of project tools, project policies, procedures, templates, and other shared documentation. In addition, the PMO manages communication across projects; monitors project timelines, budget, and quality on an enterprise level; and provides a mentoring platform for project managers.

# IT Projects

IT projects are projects involving information technology (IT) organizations. Extensive research and practical experience have shown that not all tasks in the various phases of a non-IT project are equivalent to the tasks and activities of an IT project. In an IT environment, the deliverable is often intangible (such as in a software application). Also, designers are often the implementers. IT departments often have multiple projects going on simultaneously that are linked. The initiation and success of one project might depend on the successful completion of another project. Scope creep is another factor, as is the constantly changing IT environment. Decision makers often read about a new technology and want to add it to a project without understanding what kind of effect their request will have on the project. This scenario is in contrast to managing a construction project (from which much of the prevailing project management theory is derived), where the work is linear and roles are clearly delineated.

## Project Management Software

Project management software is any number of computer applications used to manage a project schedule and resources. Some examples of project management software are Microsoft Project, Oracle Primavera, and Artemis Views. These types of tools give the project manager the ability to plan and track a project's progress. To use such tools effectively, the project manager must have a sound understanding of project management processes and procedures. Choosing the appropriate tool depends on the project's complexity, the project manager's level of experience with the software, and specific organizational standards. There might be certain project management tools your organization will mandate that you use.

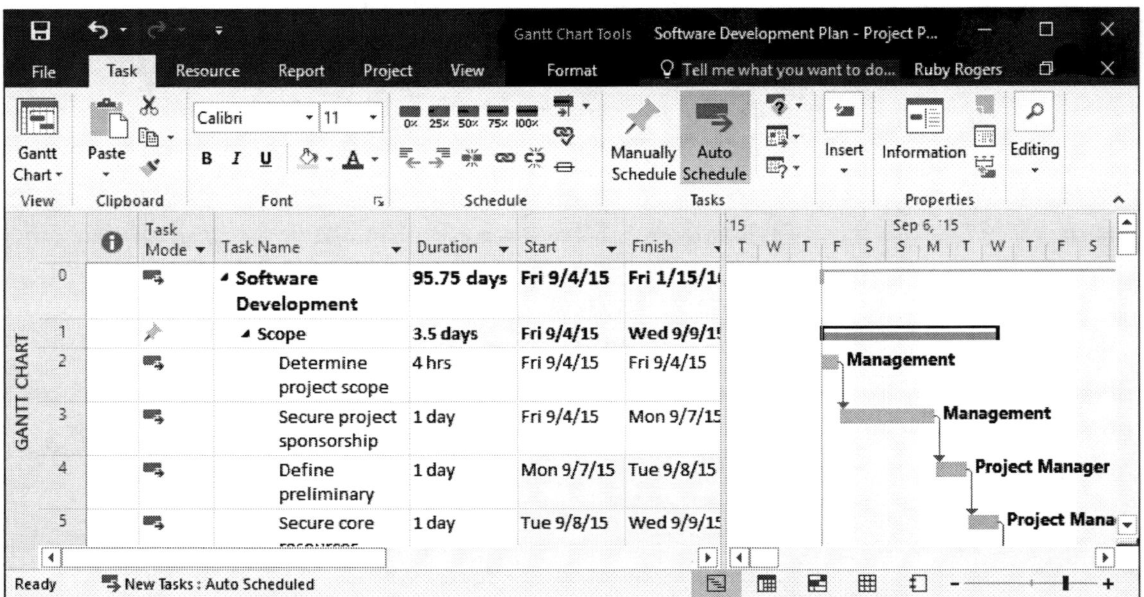

*Figure 1-6: Microsoft Project is an example of project management software.*

## Guidelines for Identifying the Role of a Project Manager

 **Note:** All Guidelines for this lesson are available as checklists from the **Checklist** tile on the CHOICE Course screen.

The overall success of a project depends largely on the role played by the project manager.

### Identify the Role of a Project Manager

To be effective as a project manager, follow these guidelines:

- Apply project management knowledge to formalize project management.
  - Use project management tools and techniques to manage project activities.
  - Ensure that the project team follows standard processes.
  - Identify best practices and bring them into effect.
  - Ensure that the deliverables in each phase are acceptable.
- Apply knowledge of the application area to manage technical challenges.
  - Assess the technical competency of the project team, identify areas of concern, and train the team if required.

- Ensure that the project meets accepted standards and regulations.
- Apply general management skills to successfully manage and control process responsibilities.
    - Manage the overall schedule of the project to ensure its successful completion on time.
    - Coordinate resources and motivate them to work towards the success of the project.
    - Identify and manage issues that arise in the project.
    - Monitor the project continuously to ensure that it meets the quality requirements.
    - Monitor project costs and ensure that the project is completed within budget.
- Apply knowledge of the project environment to assess the impact of the project on the organization.
    - Identify the impact of the project on the physical environment.
    - Identify the impact of the project on the organization's strategic plans.
    - Identify laws that could affect the project and take steps to minimize the impact.
- Apply interpersonal skills to successfully manage responsibilities of the resources.
    - Proactively communicate project information to the project team and the stakeholders.
    - Lead the team by clearly communicating your expectations.
    - Build the team as a disciplined unit that is focused on achieving the requirements of the project.
    - Resolve conflicts that may arise in the project.
- Take on additional responsibilities such as managing multiple projects or taking charge of all the documentation of a project.

# ACTIVITY 1–3
## Identifying the Role of a Project Manager

### Scenario

Your company, Develetech, has taken up the task of developing a mobile game application based on a cooking reality television show, and you have been officially assigned as the manager for this project. A celebrity chef, Steve Jones, has been hired to provide input on the design as well as act in the video and voice segments for the game. The project has already raised expectations in the market because Jones is a famous TV personality. The project team will also include previous contestants, television writers, software developers, testers, and graphic designers.

1. **What skills do you require to ensure that the team is not bogged down by the market expectations and the celebrity of Steve Jones? (Choose two.)**

   ☐ Culinary skills

   ☐ Good communication and negotiation skills

   ☐ Ability to motivate the team

   ☐ Complete project management knowledge

2. **As a software project, what IT project considerations might complicate the progress?**

3. **The development team involves resources who perform different functions. Which organizational structure will give you the greatest control over the entire team?**

   ○ Composite

   ○ Functional

   ○ Matrix

   ○ Projectized

4. **Steve Jones's TV schedule may frequently interfere with your project's schedules and affect the working hours of the other resources. What roles do you need to play to resolve this problem? (Choose two.)**

   ☐ Manage the overall schedule of the project so that Jones's TV schedules do not hamper the successful completion of the project.

   ☐ Proactively communicate project information to the project team and the stakeholders.

   ☐ Coordinate resources and motivate them to work toward the success of the project, in spite of the issues about the availability of the chef.

   ☐ Identify the impact of the project on the organization's strategic plans.

# Summary

In this lesson, you identified the key elements of project management. This enables you to enhance your chances of success in managing a wide range of projects across application areas and industries.

**Who are the stakeholders in the project you are currently working on? What are their expectations from the project?**


**What organizational structure does your company follow? What is the project manager's level of authority?**

**Note:** Check your CHOICE Course screen for opportunities to interact with your classmates, peers, and the larger CHOICE online community about the topics covered in this course or other topics you are interested in. From the Course screen you can also access available resources for a more continuous learning experience.

# 2 | Initiating a Project

**Lesson Time: 1 hour**

## Lesson Introduction

You have some knowledge of the project life cycle and the skills required to be a project manager. Having understood the rudiments of project management, you are ready to get going with the initial stages of a project. In this lesson, you'll discover how to initiate a project and perform the critical steps involved in laying the foundation for your project's success.

Starting a project is like starting a new job; the more you know about the company, your team members, and what is expected of you, the more likely you are to hit the ground running and make a good impression. Ensuring that your project starts out right will not only save you time and resources, but will also eliminate the need to backtrack once your project is officially underway.

## Lesson Objectives

In this lesson, you will:

- Create a project scope statement.

- Identify the skills for a project team.

- Identify the risks to a project.

# TOPIC A

# Determine the Scope of a Project

You are aware of the organizational objectives, business requirements, and the expected results of a project. Now, you are ready to initiate your project. Before you begin the planning process, you need to clearly identify the tasks involved in a project. In this topic, you will determine the scope of a project.

Clearly stating the work involved in a project helps the stakeholders to understand what needs to be accomplished to meet the project's objectives. Without that, they could end up spending valuable time and resources on work that isn't even supposed to be part of their project. With a clear scope statement, you will enable all participants and stakeholders to focus on the true goals of the project.

## Scope Statements

The *scope statement* is an itemized definition of the outcome of a project. It is derived from the information provided by the stakeholders of the project. It explains what is to be included and excluded from a project. The scope can change during the course of the project.

### Scope Statement

| Version | Primary Author | Description of Version | Date Revised |
|---------|----------------|------------------------|--------------|
| Draft 1 | PM Name | Initial draft | 6/11/2016 |
| Final | PM Name | Revised from stakeholders' review | 6/30/2016 |

I. **Project Name**
Research Project for Transportation of Goods

II. **Authorities**
    A. **Project Sponsor**    B. **Project Manager**
    Ruby Rogers

III. **Description of Product/Service Characteristics:**
- The report will contain all of the deliverables listed under Part A of 'Project Deliverables and Exclusions' section
- The report will be easily readable and will be delivered in both spreadsheet and PDF formats

IV. **Project Deliverables and Exclusions**
    A. **The Research Project team will produce the following deliverables:**
- Recommendation on the most cost-effective route to transport finished goods from China to U.S.
- Complete detail on the route including modes and cost
- List of challenges, risks, and constraints in the given route
- List of potential logistics companies that the client could partner with for the purpose of cost-effective transport
- Research methods/calculations will be provided as an appendix to the main report

**Project Exclusions**

    B. **The Research Project team will NOT produce the following deliverables:**
- Transport the finished goods
- Negotiate for cost reduction with potential logistics companies

V. **Project Objectives**
- Identify and recommend the most cost-effective route to transport finished goods from China to U.S.
- Should include complete coverage of all the parameters including modes and cost along with the detailed research methods and calculations
- Project should be delivered by 09/30/2016 at a cost of $150K

**Project Outcome**

VI. **Supporting Detail**
    A. **Constraints**
- Project must be completed by end of September 2016 to enable the client to make further decisions
- Modes and routes of transport must allow potential flammable and/or restricted cargo (fireworks)
    B. **Assumptions**
- Pay-per-use subscription and paid reports will cover the necessary data required for the research
- Resources with necessary skills and expertise will be available for the duration of the project

VII. **Approval**

| | |
|---|---|
| Original signature stored with project files | 7/30/2016 |
| Ruby Rogers, Project Sponsor | Date Signed |

**Project Deliverables**

*Figure 2–1: A scope statement defines the deliverables, exclusions, and expected outcome of a project.*

## Scope Creep

*Scope creep* is the additional task items that are added to a project as the project progresses, and these items make it more difficult to achieve project goals. The PMBOK® (Project Management Body of Knowledge) defines scope creep as "The uncontrolled expansion to product or project scope without adjustments to time, cost, and resources."

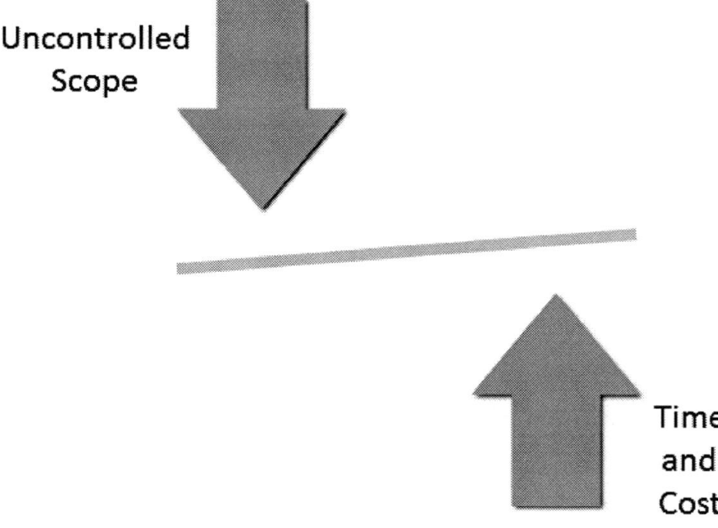

*Figure 2-2: As scope increases, cost and time must increase.*

## Constraining Factors

Constraining factors are the factors that limit the way a project can be approached. These limitations may concern time, cost, scope, quality, resources, and others. Of these, scope, cost, and time are considered as the three major constraining factors in every project. These factors are interrelated and exist in a state of equilibrium. As the project progresses, if one of these factors is altered, the other two factors should be balanced to accommodate the change without compromising the quality of the product or service.

 **Note:** The constraints are commonly referred to as the "Triple Constraints."

*Figure 2-3: The constraints form a triangle, which affects the quality of the project.*

## Project Assumptions

*Project assumptions* are statements that must be taken to be true in order for the project planning to begin. The project manager creates a list of assumptions for a project. The project benefits if the assumptions prove to be true and suffers if the assumptions are wrong. Therefore, as the project progresses, assumptions have to be reviewed and reworked to decide if they prove to be true.

### Examples of Common Project Assumptions

Some examples of common project assumptions are:

- Project staff resources will be available as and when they are needed.
- Technical support will be available as and when they are needed.
- The scope of the project will remain unchanged.

# Project Objectives

*Project objectives* are the criteria used to measure whether a project is successful or not. Objectives must be:

- Realistic and attainable.
- Specific in terms of scope.
- Quantifiable in terms of time, cost, and quality.
- Consistent with organizational plans, policies, and procedures.

Projects may have one or several objectives, and subobjectives may be added to the project in order to further clarify the project goals.

### Example: Objectives of an Add-in Component Project

The following objective was developed for a project on the development of an add-in component to a word processor application.

Develop an add-in component to the word processor application that provides advanced text-to-speech functions by October 31, 2017 at a cost of $20 for existing customers who already own a license to the application.

- The objective specifies the scope: Add-in component to a word processor application that provides advanced text-to-speech functions.
- Time: Development to be completed by October 31, 2017.
- Cost: $20 per component.

# The Scope Definition Process

The *scope definition process* allows project managers to document the project's parameters, its objectives, requirements, and deliverables in the project scope statement. There are several stages in this process.

| Stage | Description |
| --- | --- |
| Step 1: Identify Project Requirements | The first step in determining the scope of a project is requirements identification. Here the project managers obtain first hand information on the requirements from the stakeholders. Once the requirements are clearly stated, they are evaluated and then further validated against resource availability, business needs, internal contingency, and other factors that influence the scope of the project. |
| Step 2: Define Project Objectives | In this stage, the stakeholders will define what should be the outcome of the project. Objectives are clearly laid out so that they can be monitored and assessed at every level of the project life cycle. |

| **Stage** | **Description** |
|---|---|
| Step 3: Create Scope Statement | The project scope statement will be defined at this stage. Some of the essential criteria included in a project scope statement are:<br><br>• Details of contract<br>• Project objectives and requirements<br>• Scope of the project<br>• Project timeline<br>• Project milestones and deliverables<br>• Cost estimation<br>• Compensation and payment<br>• Roles and responsibilities of the people involved in the project<br>• Terms and conditions, if any<br>• Signature block |
| Step 4: Scope Sign-off | In this stage, the scope statement is sent to all the stakeholders, sponsors, and contractors for an official approval, where the scope statement is read in its entirety by all the parties involved and then signed by all parties. |

# Project Charter

The *project charter* is a document that provides a clear and concise description of the business needs that the project is intended to address. It makes a project official; it authorizes the project manager to lead the project and draw on organizational resources as needed. The project charter documents initial assumptions about the project, any known constraints, and the expected results of the project.

# Statement of Work

A *Statement Of Work (SOW)* is a document that describes the products or services that a project will supply. It specifies the work that will be done during the project and defines the business need that it is designed to meet. The SOW describes the product or service requirements and characteristics as well as the project scope and strategic plan. In addition, this document specifies the relationship between the business need and the product or service being created or provided to meet that need.

## Example: SOW for Advertising Billboards Project

Whereas the SOW describes everything from the beginning to the end of a planned work, the project charter only describes the tasks involved in a particular aspect of a job. For instance, consider an advertising agency whose core competence lies in content creation for billboards. While the agency uses its staff for creating content for a billboard, it may also procure contracts from external sources for some of the work considered necessary but beyond its core capabilities, such as specialized printing and professional photography services. The project manager is required to create a SOW specifying how management will get the overall work done and also to create project charters for each of the tasks outsourced.

# Common Project Problems

Problems faced during a project can derail its progress. Common project problems stem from poorly understood success criteria, which should be established and shared during the initial stages of the project so that they do not arise in the later stages of the project when the cost of corrective action is high. The typical problems faced in any project are:

• Uncontrolled changes in the scope of the project.
• Misunderstood deliverables.

- Overworked or underworked resources.
- Inappropriate schedules or budgets.
- Dissatisfied customers or stakeholders.

# Guidelines for Creating a Project Scope Statement

 **Note:** All Guidelines for this lesson are available as checklists from the **Checklist** tile on the CHOICE Course screen.

An effective scope statement provides a high-level definition of a project and a basis for project stakeholders to make future decisions about the project's scope.

## Create a Project Scope Statement

To create an effective project scope statement, follow these guidelines:

- Justify the need for the project.
- Clearly and concisely describe the critical characteristics and functionality of the project's product or service and the approach the team will take to achieve the project goals.
  - Ask questions to key stakeholders and customers to determine the required outcome.
  - Determine the critical characteristics of the product or service.
  - Conduct product analysis activities to develop a detailed view of the end result of the product or service.
  - Conduct alternative identification activities to generate alternative ways to achieve the project goals.
- Identify and list all the project's major deliverables whose full and satisfactory delivery constitutes completion of the project.
  - Conduct brainstorming sessions to determine the major deliverables of the product or service of the project.
  - Consult subject matter experts to identify what it will take to complete the project.
  - Consult organizational policies, relevant historical information, and the project sponsor or customer to determine which project management deliverables are required.
- Identify if there are any known exclusions to the project scope. These excluded activities are considered out of scope.
- Evaluate and validate or modify the constraints and assumptions made during initiation.
- Develop one or more project objectives—the quantifiable criteria that must be met for the project to be considered successful.
- Use precise and unambiguous language.
  - Write the project scope statement in user language rather than technical language.
  - If technical terms must be used, make sure they are clearly defined to avoid misunderstandings later.
- Ensure that all key project stakeholders receive a copy of the scope statement for review.
- Reexamine the project requirements if they need to be re-prioritized with respect to the results of the stakeholder analysis.
- Refine the project objectives, deliverables, and product scope description from the initial scope statement.
- Include a revised overall cost estimate and define any cost limitations.
- Create schedule milestones so that the client and the project team have dates for setting goals and measuring progress.
- Obtain consensus and formal approval from all key project stakeholders.

# ACTIVITY 2–1
## Examining a Project Scope Statement

### Data File

C:\095015Data\Initiating a Project\Scope_Statement.docx

### Scenario

You are a new project manager at a logistics consulting company. You have been asked to assist on a new project to help a client determine the best way to ship an order of custom fireworks from China to their location in the United States. Your manager has forwarded the scope statement document to you in an email. You need to examine the scope statement to better understand the project.

---

1. Open **Scope_Statement.docx**.
   a) Navigate to the folder containing your class files, **C:\095015Data\Initiating a Project**.
   b) Double-click **Scope_Statement.docx** to open it.

2. Examine the sections of the document and listen as your instructor summarizes each one.

3. **Which of the following are out of scope for the project? (Choose two.)**
   - ☐ The actual transportation of the fireworks.
   - ☐ A detailed report of the recommended route and modes of transportation.
   - ☐ Negotiation of reduced costs with potential logistics companies.
   - ☐ An appendix containing the details of the research and calculations.

4. **Which is a constraint to the project?**
   - ○ Contract approval
   - ○ Modes of recommended transport must allow fireworks
   - ○ Cost of transport
   - ○ Page limit set for the report

5. **True or False? Things that limit the handling of a project are called constraints?**
   - ☐ True
   - ☐ False

6. **True or False? Objectives of a project need not necessarily be measurable.**
   - ☐ True
   - ☐ False

7. **Which of the following should be captured while examining the scope of the project? (Choose three.)**
   - ☐ Project assumptions
   - ☐ The ways in which the project team will accomplish its objectives
   - ☐ The benefits that the project will have for the organization
   - ☐ Project constraints

---

# TOPIC B

# Identify the Skills for a Project Team

You outlined a well-defined scope statement and also identified the assumptions and objectives in a project. Your next step is to start the project with a team that befits the project objectives, which will in turn help you to form the ideal team to accomplish the goals of the project. In this topic, you will identify the skills for a project team.

People make projects happen. You may be well-versed in many aspects of project management, but you're not going to succeed if you can't put the right players on your team. Identifying the skillsets of the team members will increase your chances of finding the best possible people for your project.

## Project Team

A *project team* is a group of individuals who collectively have the skills required to complete a project. Every member of the project team possesses distinct skillsets and contributes collectively through the life of the project to achieve a common goal. The members of a project team may belong to different functional teams. The project team is headed by a project manager who is often selected by the stakeholders. Usually, project teams work together only for a defined period.

### Example: An Insurance Marketing Team

Susan Williams is a project manager in an insurance company. She is responsible for marketing a wide range of new insurance schemes. She identifies the skills required for her team and decides that she needs a market specialist, designers for preparing presentations and hand bills, and a few volunteers to help her distribute pamphlets and answer customer queries.

## Project Team Members

The members of a project team include core team members and implementation team members. The core team members are key individuals who work on the major activities that the team will undertake during the project, whereas the implementation team members are individuals who carry out activities planned by the core team members. The members of the project team grow during the implementation phase of the project. Some of the implementation team members stay with the team for a short span of time, while others stay throughout the entire implementation phase. The core team members stay throughout the life of a project.

## Virtual Project Teams

Project teams need not necessarily be located in the same geographical area. They can be scattered in different locations but still be a part of the project team by communicating through tools such as the phone, instant messaging, online meeting, and Voice over Internet connections. The primary reasons for forming virtual teams are organizational expectations and personal flexibility of the team members. However, there may be other reasons. Some of the key qualities required of a virtual project team are:

- Knowledge of the team members.
- Trust and respect for the team members.
- Ability to communicate effectively with the team members.
- Willingness to share project status information with the team members through email or phone regularly or periodically.

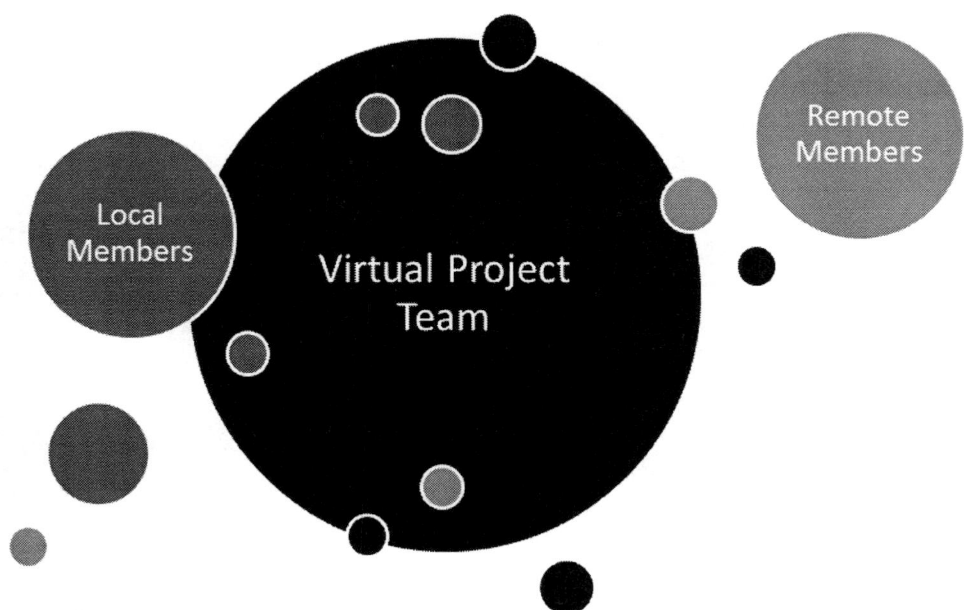


*Figure 2-4: A virtual team is prone to risks such as lack of proper interaction between the team members, time zone differences, misinterpretation due to differences in language, and technological incompatibility.*

# Team Skills Matrix

The *team skills matrix* helps you to identify the team members you need to perform the tasks in a project. It includes a listing of the skills required to complete the project tasks and the level of skill required to accomplish those tasks. In addition, it includes a list of selection criteria that helps you determine whether team members possess those skills. Based on the skill requirements matching, you can select the members for the project team. A meticulously prepared skills matrix helps you in the selection of team members or in the identification of missing skills in the current team.

## Example: Team Skills Matrix for a Database Project

| Skills | Skill Level Required for the Job | Supervision Required for the Job | Experience Level Required for the Job | Education Level Required for the Job | Team Member |
|---|---|---|---|---|---|
| Data Architect | Design overall schema and database architecture | Work without supervision | Minimum 5 years as data architect | Masters in computer science or equivalent | Sanjay Joshi |
| Database Developer | Write stored procedures and SQL scripts to implement database | Ability to work unsupervised but also under supervision of Data Architect | Minimum 5 years professional database development | B.S. or equivalent | Nicole Robinson |

| Skills | Skill Level Required for the Job | Supervision Required for the Job | Experience Level Required for the Job | Education Level Required for the Job | Team Member |
|---|---|---|---|---|---|
| QA Engineer | Develop automated and manual tests to ensure the accuracy and efficiency of database implementation | Unsupervised | Minimum 3 years database testing | B.S. or equivalent | Caitlin Nolan |

 **Access the Checklist tile on your CHOICE Course screen for reference information and job aids on How to Identify the Skills for a Project Team.**

# ACTIVITY 2-2
## Identifying Skills Using the Skills Matrix

### Scenario

In your role as project manager at Develetech, you have developed the team skills matrix for the cooking reality show game application. You now need to determine how to handle the resource requirements for the project.

| Skills | Skill Level Required for the Job | Supervision Required for the Job | Experience Level Required for the Job | Education Level Required for the Job | Team Member |
|---|---|---|---|---|---|
| Head Chef | Main celebrity talent, able to react to game scenarios with authenticity, excellent acting and voice over skills | Work under the supervision of video director and audio producer | Minimum 2 years as celebrity reality show head chef and judge | Culinary certificate | Steve Jones |
| Audio producer | Produce recorded voice overs for game characters; must be proficient in recording tools and directing talent | Ability to work unsupervised | Minimum 5 years professional audio | | |
| Video director | Produce video segments of actors for incorporation into game | Unsupervised | Minimum 3 years, game industry desirable | | Jen Baker |
| Editor/Effects Design | Produce game ready video and animation assets; must be proficient in technical toolset | Unsupervised | Minimum 5 years creating moving assets | Certificate in toolset desired but not required | Tom Wu |

| Skills | Skill Level Required for the Job | Supervision Required for the Job | Experience Level Required for the Job | Education Level Required for the Job | Team Member |
|---|---|---|---|---|---|
| Lead Developer | Lead team of contracted developers; drive architecture of application and development methods; extensive experience in game application development | Unsupervised | Minimum 10 years in development, at least 5 in gaming | B.S. in computer science or equivalent work experience | Maria Ruiz |
| Developers | TBD based on toolset/ platforms | Supervised | Will vary | B.S. or equivalent experience | |

1. If you were the project manager for the project, how would you respond to the blank spaces?

2. The video director, Jen Baker, is not in a position to continue in the team due to unavoidable circumstances. The management is now contemplating the right person to take her position and complete the tasks. Who do you think might be the right person to replace Jen Baker?

3. True or False? Based on the empty spaces in the matrix, you need to hire an audio producer and developers.
   - ☐ True
   - ☐ False

4. Which team member would be most difficult to replace?
   - ○ Tom Wu
   - ○ Steve Jones
   - ○ Maria Ruiz
   - ○ Jen Baker

5. What are the uses of a team skills matrix? (Choose three.)
   - ☐ Identify the availability of team members.
   - ☐ Identify which team members have the required skillsets.
   - ☐ Break out skills needed for each project task.
   - ☐ Identify criteria that may be used to determine whether a team member has a particular skillset.

# TOPIC C

# Identify the Risks to a Project

You took considerable effort to determine the scope of the project so that you can get the project started. You now need to spot and tackle the problems which may arise during the course of your project. In this topic, you will identify the risks involved in a project.

Unexpected events can upset your work plan or bring your project to a halt. Identifying risks early helps you to reduce their severity. Risk identifying allows you to be proactive in your approach towards problems, rather than scrambling to respond to problems.

## Risk

A *risk* is an uncertain event that may have a positive or negative effect on a project. Its primary components are a measure of probability that a risk will occur and the impact of the risk on a project. In project management, the risk that matters is anything that might negatively impact the project's completion on time, within the defined scope and budget, while conforming to the predefined quality standards.

### Example: Risks in a Project Involving Production of Promotional Materials

Sheila, a bank manager, is acting as a project manager, overseeing the production of new promotional materials for her bank's mortgage division. Sheila hires independent contractors, including a graphic designer, copywriter, and commercial printer. She wants the materials produced soon, but she recognizes that the risks include increased costs in rush printing fees and a greater probability of errors because the job is being pushed quickly through its production cycle.

 **Note:** To learn more about web application vulnerabilities, check out the LearnTO **Identify Project Risks** presentation from the **LearnTO** tile on the CHOICE Course screen.

## Impact of Risk Over Time

Project risks progress over time. The probability of risk over an event is minimal during the initial stage of a project; therefore, risk controlled effectively during this stage can prove to be cost-effective. The impact of risk over time multiplies as the project progresses, when the possibility of meeting the project's planned scope, time, and budget becomes more difficult.

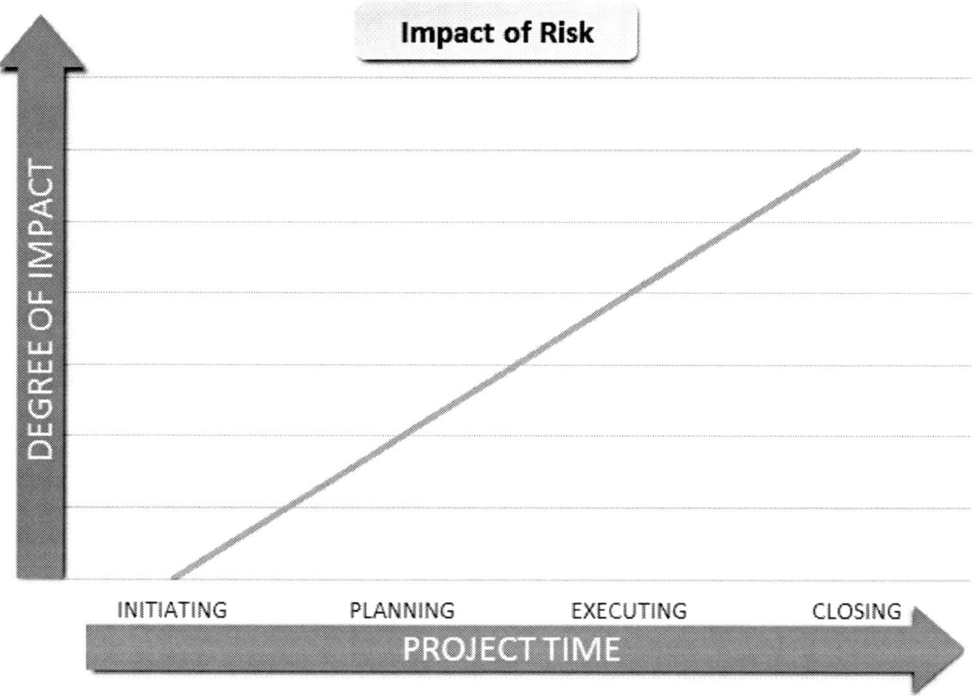


*Figure 2–5: Progression of risk over time reinforces the importance of planning.*

# Guidelines for Identifying the Risks to a Project

Identifying and documenting risks helps you plan for risks that might affect the project development. Follow these guidelines to identify the risks to a project.

## Identify the Risks to a Project

To identify project risks, follow these guidelines:

- Determine the potential people risks associated with a project.
    - Will team members be available when needed?
    - Do they understand the project's purpose and objectives?
    - Can they work together?
- Determine the technology-based risks associated with the project.
    - Does the team have the right skills?
    - Are the tools and software available appropriate? robust? scalable?
- Determine the organization-based risks associated with the project.
    - Do all stakeholders agree on project objectives and purpose?
    - Are there stakeholders who have not participated in initiating the project?
    - Does the sponsor have enough clout to influence other stakeholders?
- Determine the finance-based risks associated with the project.
    - Will the project manager require multiple sign-offs before spending money? If so, how much time will they take and what is the scheduling impact?
    - Will currency fluctuations impact availability of cash?
    - Does ongoing funding depend on the timeliness of the client's progress payments?
- Determine the law- or contract-based risks associated with the project.
    - Are pending regulatory issues likely to impact project specifications?
    - Do suppliers own the patent for the technology you expect to purchase?
- Determine the physical-based risks associated with the project.

- Are workers more likely to get hurt if you increase the number of hours they work?
  - Has your company undertaken fire prevention measures?
- Determine the environment-based risks associated with the project.
  - How will an early hurricane season impact the project?
  - Will environmental pollution impact the clean room air quality?
  - Will municipal construction projects impact the productivity?
- Look out for special circumstances that might arise in any project segment.
- Consult relevant historical information from previous, similar projects that may include lessons learned describing problems and their resolutions.

# ACTIVITY 2–3
## Identifying Sources of Risk

### Scenario

As a project manager working for Develetech, you are ready to identify some possible risks of the Steve Jones reality show game application project. Based on what you know so far about the project, you begin to brainstorm some potential sources of risk.

1. Spend a few minutes brainstorming with your group some of the obvious project risks. Make sure to record these for use in later activities.

2. There may be risks that you have not yet identified. Use the following risk category list to prompt your group to think of more risks and add them to your list: Budget/funding, Schedule, Changes to scope/requirements, Technical issues, Personnel issues, Hardware, Contracts, and Political/legal concerns.

# Summary

In this lesson, you explored the significant elements of initiating a project, which is one of the primary processes and a critical part of every project. By effectively initiating a project and laying a solid foundation for the work that will follow, you will significantly increase your chances for success.

**Consider the benefits of developing a project scope statement. How do you anticipate using this process to your advantage in your next project?**

**What do you think is the significance of risk identification and what lessons on risk identification will you offer to others?**

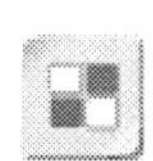

**Note:** Check your CHOICE Course screen for opportunities to interact with your classmates, peers, and the larger CHOICE online community about the topics covered in this course or other topics you are interested in. From the Course screen you can also access available resources for a more continuous learning experience.

# 3 | Planning for Time and Cost

**Lesson Time: 1 hour, 30 minutes**

## Lesson Introduction

You initiated a project and identified the skills required to perform the project tasks. Now that you have a solid foundation to start the project, you need to plan for its successful completion. In this lesson, you will plan for the project time and cost.

The ability to deliver projects on time and within budget is the cornerstone of good project management. By identifying the methods of creating accurate duration, resources, and cost estimates that will guide your projects, you can meet the expectations and deliver the desired results.

## Lesson Objectives

In this lesson, you will:

- Create a Work Breakdown Structure.

- Sequence the activities.

- Create a project schedule.

- Determine project costs.

# TOPIC A

## Create a WBS

You created a project scope statement and identified the skills required for the project team. The next logical step will be to identify the smaller tasks in the project that can be assigned to the individual team members. In this topic, you will create a work breakdown structure.

It's always easier to successfully complete a project by breaking it down into smaller, more manageable chunks. Creating an effective work breakdown structure helps you schedule the project work and create accurate time, cost, and resource estimates.

### WBS

The *Work Breakdown Structure (WBS)* is a hierarchical structure that subdivides project work into smaller, more manageable pieces of work. The work defined in the WBS maps to the project's scope statement, and it has to be executed by the project team to accomplish the project objectives. A WBS helps to identify project deliverables. It provides an increasingly detailed definition of the project work at each descending level, with the lowest-level components, called work packages, containing components of work that can be scheduled, cost estimated, monitored, and controlled. The level of detail of the work packages will vary depending on the size and complexity of the project.

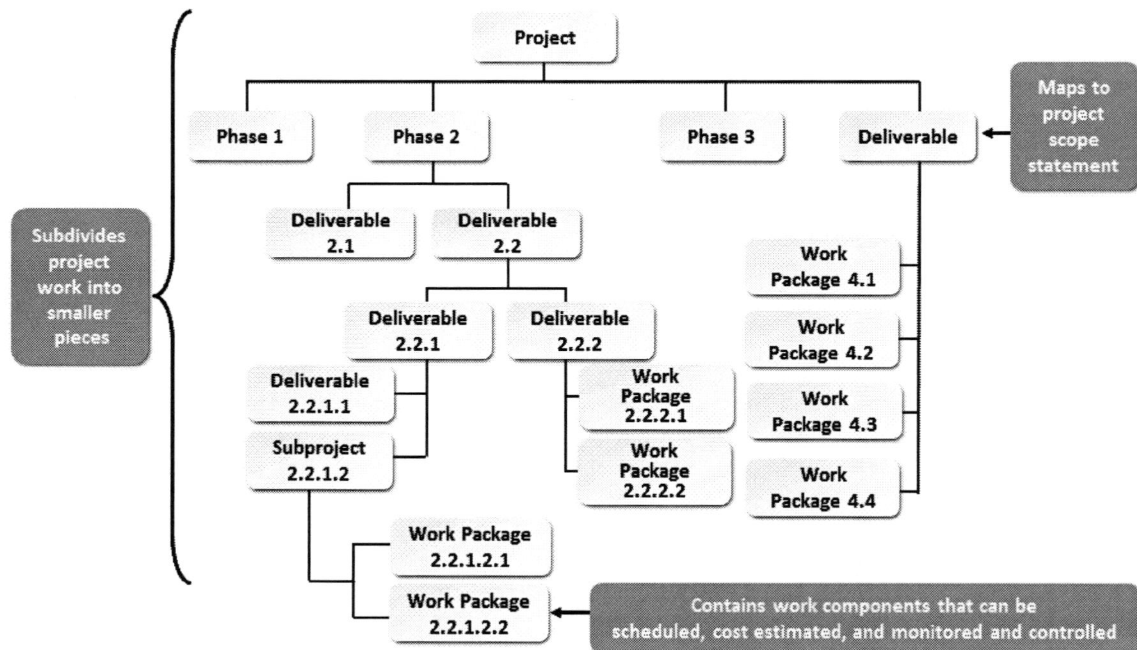


*Figure 3-1: Work Breakdown Structure.*

## Decomposition

*Decomposition* is a technique for creating the WBS by subdividing project work to the work package level. An analysis of the scope statement will help to identify the project work. The level of decomposition varies for different projects. Decomposition of a project work is stopped when the components of the work packages are sufficient to complete the work and can be assigned to an individual, cost estimated, scheduled, and monitored.

 **Access the Checklist tile on your CHOICE Course screen for reference information and job aids on How to Create a Work Breakdown Structure.**

## ACTIVITY 3–1
## Creating a Work Breakdown Structure

### Data File

C:\095015Data\Planning for Time and Cost\Work_Breakdown_Structure.docx

### Scenario

The game application team at Develetech is expected to create an initial design document with visual samples for the cooking reality show game application. The first draft will include the technical requirements, game play overview, high-level storyboard, and sample screenshots of key elements. You now want to create a WBS for this deliverable.

1. Working with your group, create a list of the work packages that make up this deliverable.

2. Spend a few minutes decomposing a few of the items you listed as work packages. Write out some of the tasks that may be needed to complete the items. Be sure to consider tasks that need to happen before deliverable work can begin, such as research, purchasing hardware, interviews, and so on.

3. Open **Work_Breakdown_Structure.docx**.
   a) Navigate to the folder containing your class files, **C:\095015Data\Initiating a Project**.
   b) Double-click **Work_Breakdown_Structure.docx** to open it.

4. Enter the deliverables and tasks into the WBS. Create a high-level task for three of the deliverables to enter on lines 1, 2, and 3 (for example, Develop Technical Requirements). List some of the tasks you identified in Step 2 under each of the deliverables.

# TOPIC B

# Sequence the Activities

You have created a work breakdown structure and identified the activities in a project. Before you begin to develop a project plan for scheduling the activities, you need to identify the order in which the individual activities need to be performed. In this topic, you will sequence the activities.

Identifying the activities in a project and the relationships between them is a fundamental step for determining the order in which the activities need to be performed. Careful sequencing of the activities will ensure that the project progresses towards its successful completion.

## Activity

An *activity* is a unit of project work that must be performed to complete a project deliverable. Every activity has a duration and cost, and consumes resources. Activities occur at the lowest level of the work breakdown structure. An activity takes inputs to perform the work required and produces outputs that may serve as inputs to another activity. Activities differ in the complexity of work involved, the duration required to complete them, the resources they require, the cost involved, the outputs they produce, and their criticality to successful project completion. Activities are commonly referred to as tasks in project management.

## Activity Sequencing

*Activity sequencing* involves identifying and documenting the relationships among activities, and arranging the activities in a sequence based on those relationships. Identification of relationships helps to determine the correct order in which the activities need to be performed. A correct sequence of activities is essential for the development of an achievable project plan. Activity sequencing can be carried out using project management software, manual techniques, or a combination of both.

## Dependencies

An *activity dependency* is a logical relationship between two activities that indicates whether the start of one activity depends upon an event or input from another activity or an external factor. There are three types of dependencies.

| Type | Description |
| --- | --- |
| Mandatory | Inherent in the nature of the project work. Activities are presumed to have a mandatory dependency if they have to be performed in a particular sequence for the work to be completed successfully.<br>**Example:** Books can't be bound before they're printed. |
| Discretionary | Established by the project manager if there are no mandatory or external dependencies between the activities. The project manager applies the application area's best practices and uses his or her previous experience to decide on the sequence of the activities.<br>**Example:** The sponsor would like to see the book's cover design as soon as possible, so the team may decide to have the cover artwork done before the inside illustrations. |

| Type | Description |
| --- | --- |
| External | An event or input outside the project activities that dictates the sequence of the activities.<br>**Example:** Books can't be printed until the shipment of paper arrives. |

# Precedence Relationships

A *precedence relationship* is a logical relationship between two activities that indicates which activity should be performed first and which one should be performed later. The activity that is performed first is called the predecessor activity, and the one that is performed later is called the successor activity.

There are four types of precedence relationships.

| Type | Description |
| --- | --- |
| Finish-to-Start | The precedence relationship in which the predecessor activity must finish before the successor activity can start.<br>**Example:** The foundation for the house must be finished (Activity A) before the framing can start (Activity B). |
| Finish-to-Finish | The precedence relationship in which the predecessor activity must finish before the successor activity can finish.<br>**Example:** Construction must be finished (Activity A) before the building inspection can be finished (Activity B). |
| Start-to-Start | The precedence relationship in which the predecessor activity must start before the successor activity can start.<br>**Example:** The building design must start (Activity A) before the electrical layout design can start (Activity B). |
| Start-to-Finish | The precedence relationship in which the predecessor activity must start before the successor activity can finish.<br>**Example:** The electrical inspections must start (Activity A) before you can finish the drywalling (Activity B). |

# Project Schedule Network Diagrams

A *project schedule network diagram* is a graphical representation of the activities in a project and the logical relationships between those activities. There are two methods for constructing a project schedule network diagram. The Precedence Diagramming Method (PDM) is a technique for creating a project schedule network diagram in which activities are represented by boxes or rectangles, referred to as nodes, and relationships are represented by arrows connecting the nodes. The Arrow Diagramming Method (ADM) is a technique for creating a project schedule network diagram in which activities are represented by arrows, and their relationships are represented by connecting the arrows using nodes.

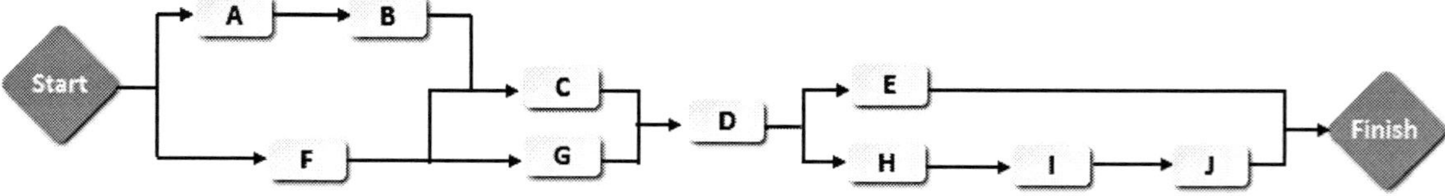


*Figure 3–2: A project schedule network diagram shows how tasks relate in order.*

# Lag

A *lag* is a modification in a logical relationship that delays the start of a successor activity. It is determined by an external or mandatory dependency and may affect activities with any of the four precedence relationships. Lag time is considered a positive value since it adds time to the overall duration of a project.

# Lead

A *lead* is a modification in a logical relationship that allows the successor activity to start before the predecessor activity ends in a Finish-to-Start relationship. A lead is implemented when you need to accelerate a successor activity in order to shorten the overall project schedule. Lead time is considered a negative value since it lessens the overall duration of a project.

 **Access the Checklist tile on your CHOICE Course screen for reference information and job aids on How to Create a Project Schedule Network Diagram.**

# ACTIVITY 3-2

## Sequencing Activities in a Project Schedule Network Diagram

### Scenario

You identified some of the activities in creating an animation in the game application project and determined the logical relationships that exist between some of them. You realize that a Finish-to-Start precedence relationship exists between the activities in the project. Using these inputs, you have started a project schedule network diagram. You need to complete diagramming the activities in the correct sequence and add a task to the diagram.

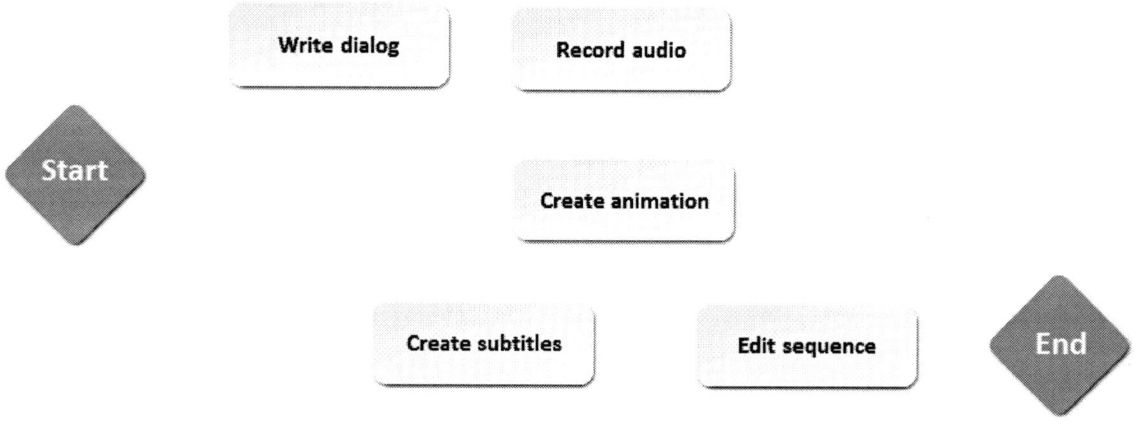


1. The animator needs to match his work to the audio. This means that the audio must be recorded before the animation can begin. How would you connect these tasks? Sketch your answer.

2. You have been informed that subtitles need to be created so that the game can be played without audio. You need to add an additional task, "Create Subtitles," to the network diagram. The animator informs you that he can create subtitles that can be edited in over the animation and he can create them as soon as the dialog is written. Which would be the most appropriate location for this task in the network diagram? Sketch your answer and sketch in all remaining connections.

3. According to the project schedule network diagram, which is the "Create animation" task's predecessor activity?
   - ○ Edit sequence
   - ○ Create subtitles
   - ○ Record audio
   - ○ Write dialog

4. What task can be done in parallel with the "Record audio" task?
   - ○ Write dialog
   - ○ Edit sequence
   - ○ Create subtitles
   - ○ None

# TOPIC C

# Create a Project Schedule

You sequenced the activities in a project. The next step is to develop a project plan for performing these activities. In this topic, you will create a project schedule.

Given the importance of the project schedule and its high visibility, you want to make sure that the schedule you create is realistic. To arrive at a project schedule that is achievable, it is important to estimate the resource availability and establish realistic start and finish dates for each activity.

## Resources

*Resources* are people, equipment, materials, or other costs that are used to accomplish a project task. In other words, resources are the staff, supplies, equipment, and other expenses that you need to execute a project.

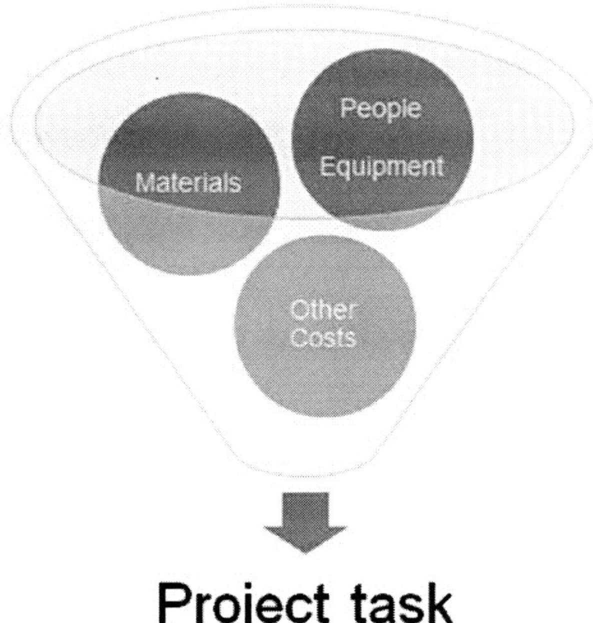


*Figure 3-3: Resources are the people, equipment, materials, and costs needed to complete project tasks.*

## Resource Estimation

*Resource estimation* is the means of determining the resources required to complete project activities. Resources refer to any useful material object or any person needed for the project work to be completed. Resource estimates specify the quantities of the resources that will be used and the period for which the resources should be available to perform the activities. Resources are almost always limited in quantity and therefore require thoughtful allocation.

## Resource Leveling

Resource leveling is a technique that assists in making scheduling decisions when there are resource management concerns. It allows you to readjust the work as appropriate so that people are not overly allocated. It is also used to address scheduling activities when critical resources are only available at certain times. For example, you may want to delay the start of an activity if the resource has other tasks scheduled for the same time or will be unavailable to complete the work.

There are several approaches to leveling:

- Increasing the duration of a task.
- Increasing the number of resources assigned to a task.
- Reassigning a task to another resource who has free time.
- Rescheduling a task.

Project managers typically use a combination of these approaches to achieve a level project.

## Duration Estimation

*Duration estimation* is the act of estimating the time periods that are required to complete project activities. To estimate durations, the scope of work of an activity, the required resources, the time periods for which the resources will be required, and the availability of resources during those time periods are taken into account. The duration estimation process calculates the amount of effort and the amount of resources required to arrive at an estimate of the time required to complete each activity. Duration estimation is performed by the project manager in consultation with the project team members who are familiar with the nature of the work to be performed.

## Schedule Development Terminologies

The schedule development terms are used to identify the key parameters of a project schedule.

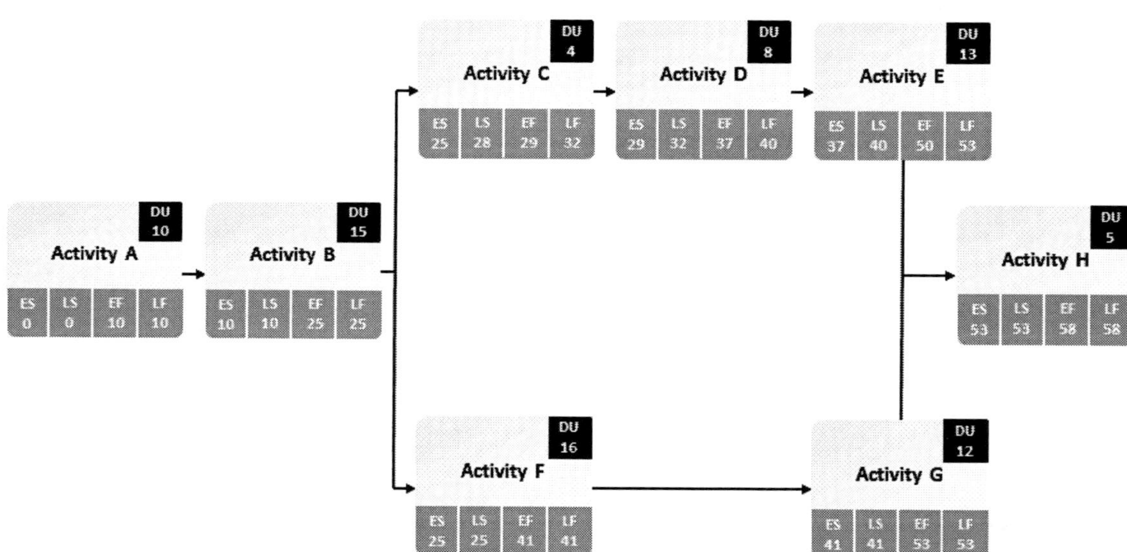


*Figure 3-4: A precedence diagram contains the values for the schedule development terms.*

| Term | Description |
| --- | --- |
| DU | Duration. The number of work periods required for the completion of an activity. |
| ES | Early start. The earliest time an activity can start. The ES of the first activity in a network diagram is zero. The ES of all other activities is the latest early finish (EF) of any predecessor activities (assuming that any successor activity starts as soon as all its predecessor activities are finished). |
| EF | Early finish. The earliest time an activity can finish. The EF for the first activity is the same as its duration. For all other activities, EF is the latest EF of all of an activity's predecessor activities plus its duration. |

| Term | Description |
| --- | --- |
| LF | Late finish. The latest time an activity can finish. The LF for the last activity is the same as its EF time. The LF for any predecessor activity is the earliest LS of any of its successor activities. |
| LS | Late start. The latest time an activity can start. The LS for the last activity is its EF minus its duration. The LS for any predecessor activity is its LF minus its duration. |

# Critical Path

*Critical path* is the path in the project schedule network diagram that has the longest duration. The duration of the critical path is calculated by adding the durations of the individual activities along the path. Activities on the critical path cannot be delayed as it will delay the whole project, unless the subsequent activities are shortened.

**Note:** A project may have more than one critical path. For example, there may be two parallel tasks with the same start, finish, and duration, both of which drive the end date equally.

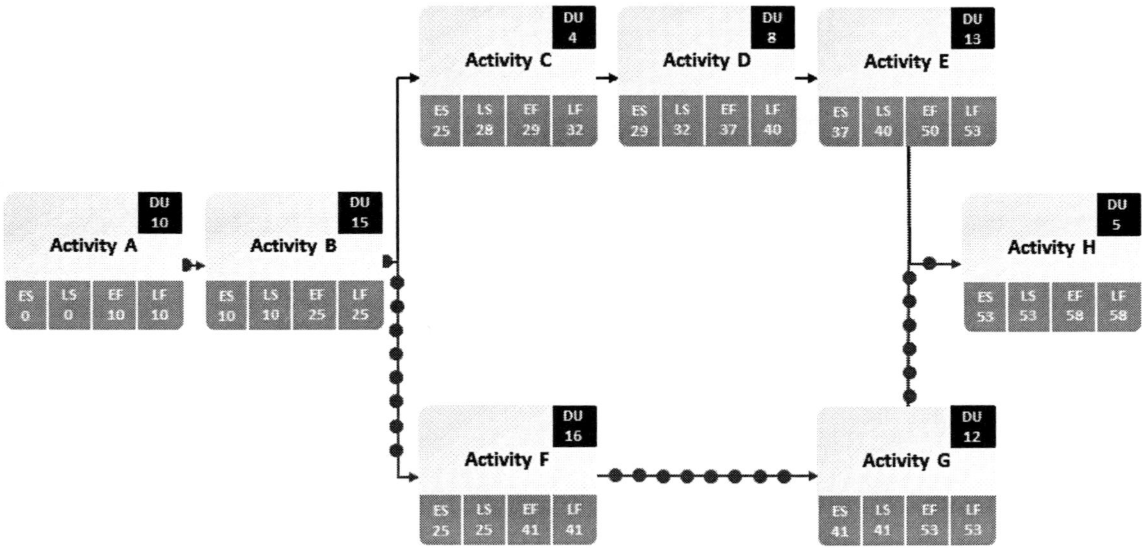

*Figure 3–5: The critical path connects the tasks that drive the end date of the project.*

**Note:** To learn more about web application vulnerabilities, check out the LearnTO **Find the Critical Path** presentation from the **LearnTO** tile on the CHOICE Course screen.

# Float

*Float* is the amount of time an activity can be delayed without delaying the ES of the immediate successor activity. *Total float* is the amount of time an activity can be delayed from its ES without delaying the project finish date. It is calculated by subtracting an activity's EF from its LF or its ES from its LS. In most cases, float has a value greater than zero only in activities that are not on the critical path. If there are two or more activities in a path with float, the total float for that string of activities is shared by all the activities in the string. If one activity uses all of the float, there's none left for the others. Float is also called slack.

## Schedule Baselines

The schedule baseline is the version of the project schedule that is approved by stakeholders and serves as the basis for measuring the project's progress. It contains the planned start and finish dates for all the activities. By comparing your project's progress to the baseline, you can determine if your project is not performing as expected and you can then take corrective action to finish the project. A baseline is essential to the monitoring and controlling function of project management.

**Access the Checklist tile on your CHOICE Course screen for reference information and job aids on How to Create a Project Schedule.**

# ACTIVITY 3-3
## Creating a Project Schedule

### Date File

C:\095015Data\Planning for Time and Cost\Project_Schedule.docx

### Scenario

You have identified the proper sequence of the project activities and completed the project schedule network diagram. You have also estimated the duration in business days of each activity. You need to identify the activities in the project that cannot be delayed and find out the early start, early finish, late start, and late finish values of all the activities in the project.

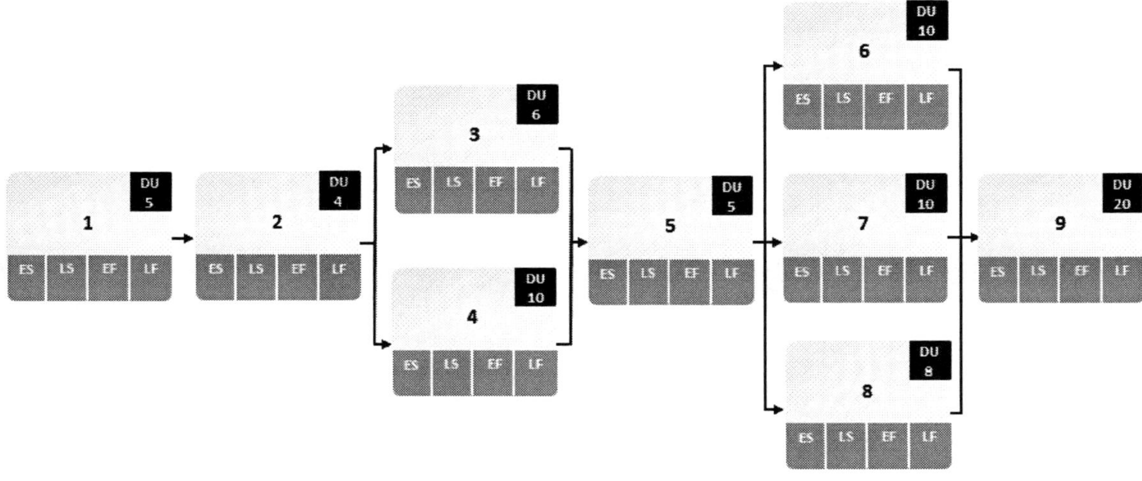

1. In the given project schedule, the ES value of Task 1 is 0 and duration is 5. What will be the calculated EF value of Task 1? Fill in the ES and EF values in the diagram provided for all the steps in this activity.

2. What will be the early start value of Task 2?

3. Calculate the early finish value of Task 2, given the early start value is 5 and duration is 4.

4. Consider the early finish value of Task 2 as 9, the duration of Task 3 as 6, and the duration of Task 4 as 10. What will be the early start and early finish values of Tasks 3 and 4?

5.  What will be the early start and early finish values for Task 5?

6.  What are the early start and early finish values of Tasks 6, 7, 8, and 9?

7.  For Task 9, the early start value is 34 and early finish value is 54. What will be the calculated late finish value of Task 9?

8.  The late finish value of Task 9 is 54. What is the late start value of Task 9?

9.  What are the late finish and late start values of Task 8?

10. What are the late finish and late start values for Tasks 6 and 7?

11. What are the late finish and late start values for Task 5?

12. What are the late finish and late start values for Tasks 1, 2, 3, and 4?

13. Which is a valid critical path for this project?
    ○  1, 2, 4, 5, 8, 9
    ○  1, 2, 3, 5, 6, 9
    ○  1, 2, 4, 5, 6, 9
    ○  1, 2, 3, 5, 8, 9

14. What is the duration of the critical path?
    ○  54
    ○  56
    ○  52
    ○  50

15. Which activities in the project do not fall on the critical path? (Choose two.)
    ☐  Task 6
    ☐  Task 4
    ☐  Task 3
    ☐  Task 8

# TOPIC D

# Determine Project Costs

You have drafted a project schedule. To arrive at an estimate of how much your project is going to cost, you need to calculate the cost involved in performing each activity in the schedule. In this topic, you will estimate project costs.

Inappropriately high cost estimates may discourage sponsors from pursuing projects that have the potential for success. Conversely, estimates that are too low could waste precious resources on a project that ultimately proves unfeasible. As a project manager, it is your responsibility to estimate project costs as accurately as possible.

## Cost Estimates

A *cost estimate* is an assessment of the likely costs of the resources required to complete an activity. It also involves identifying risks that might affect the cost required to perform the activities. It is expressed in monetary values. Historical cost information of similar projects can help a project manager in estimating costs. The accuracy of cost estimates increases as the project progresses.

### Example: Estimating Cost of a Research Project

While estimating the costs of a research project, you discuss with the research team and arrive at rough estimates for the work packages. You also determine the rates for the resources involved in the project and the technologies they will use. You also weigh the costs of outsourcing the work in the project as opposed to doing it in-house. You then identify the availability of authentic information and appropriate technologies as possible risks to the project. Finally, you review the cost estimates and submit them along with a list of assumptions that you made while arriving at those estimates.

## Cost Budgeting

*Cost budgeting* is the process of aggregating the cost estimates of all the activities or work packages to arrive at an overall cost estimate for the project. Cost budgeting also takes contract information of resources, project constraints, and risks into account while arriving at an estimate for the project. The outcome of cost budgeting serves as the foundation for monitoring project costs as the project progresses. It also serves to find out if the project will require additional funding and helps stakeholders assess the financial feasibility of the project.

## Cost Baselines

The *cost baseline* is an outcome of cost budgeting that is approved by stakeholders and serves as the basis for measuring the project's progress. It contains a summation of the estimated costs of the activities by period. You can compare the costs of the project as it progresses against the baseline to determine if your project is staying within budget and take corrective actions if necessary.

## Guidelines for Determining Project Costs

> **Note:** All Guidelines for this lesson are available as checklists from the **Checklist** tile on the CHOICE Course screen.

Accurately estimating project costs will prevent overruns and unforeseen expenditures. Follow these guidelines to determine project costs.

## Determine Project Costs

To develop accurate cost estimates, follow these guidelines:

- Involve the work package owners.
  - When possible, the cost figures that go into the cost estimates for individual work packages should be provided by those who will actually provide the resources. As always, it is the people who will do the work, provide the service, or supply the material that can best estimate what the associated costs will be. It is the project manager's responsibility to compile these cost figures into realistic estimates.
  - For some projects, though, the project manager will be solely responsible for generating the cost estimates. This may be the case for:
    - Small projects in which the project manager is very familiar with the activities required.
    - Projects with very well-defined resource requirements.
    - Projects that are very similar to past projects for which the costs are well documented.

**Note:** Even in such cases, the project manager may want to do a quick reality check with the resource supplier to make sure no incorrect assumptions have been made.

- Gather any relevant input information that may help you prepare the estimates, such as estimating publications and resource rates.
- Look for alternative costing options. Some options you might explore could include:
  - Using stock components versus custom-made.
  - Stretching the duration of an activity to eliminate overtime charges.
  - Leasing versus purchasing of capital equipment.
  - Outsourcing as opposed to handling the work in-house.
- Determine the units of measure that will be used.
  - Estimates should all be in the same unit of measure (usually monetary).
  - Units must be clearly defined and easily interpreted.
- Consider possible risks that may impact cost.
- Ensure that all cost estimates are assigned to the appropriate account, according to the chart of accounts.
- Make sure your cost estimates include the following key elements:
  - Estimated costs for all resources that will be charged to the project. Use the WBS and resource requirements document to develop the estimates.
  - The level of estimate.
  - A list of assumptions made when developing the estimates.

# ACTIVITY 3-4
## Determining Project Costs

## Scenario

In your role as project manager at Develetech, you have drafted a project schedule after sequencing the activities and estimating the resource and activity duration for the cooking reality show game application project. Now, you need to find out the cost of the individual activities and that of the project as a whole.

1. **What information does the cost estimate of an activity in the project convey?**
   - ○ The cost incurred by the activity in a similar past project.
   - ○ The planned cost of resources required to perform the activity.
   - ○ The project's budgeted cost.
   - ○ The pay received by each resource per hour.

2. **True or False? During the cost budgeting of the cooking reality show game application project, you need to take Steve Jones's contract information into account.**
   - ☐ True
   - ☐ False

3. **Upon cost budgeting the game application project, what important analyses can the stakeholders perform? (Choose two.)**
   - ☐ Assess the financial feasibility of the project.
   - ☐ Determine market demand for the application.
   - ☐ Determine additional funding requirements.
   - ☐ Identify the risks to the project.

# Summary

In this lesson, you planned for project time and cost. Planning the time and cost of a project will help you meet expectations and deliver the desired results.

**How important is the WBS in creating an effective project schedule? What is the level of decomposition you will like to achieve in order to manage your project efficiently?**

**How will the ability to estimate costs effectively improve your performance on the job?**

**Note:** Check your CHOICE Course screen for opportunities to interact with your classmates, peers, and the larger CHOICE online community about the topics covered in this course or other topics you are interested in. From the Course screen you can also access available resources for a more continuous learning experience.

# 4 | Planning for Project Risks, Communication, and Change Control

**Lesson Time: 30 minutes**

## Lesson Introduction

You have planned the time and cost for the project. Now you need to proceed with the other elements of good planning. In this lesson, you'll plan for project risks, communication, and change control in your project.

You want to make sure that none of the customers, stakeholders, or members of the project management team are surprised by delays, changes, or unavoidable risks. By planning ahead and monitoring the project, you can increase your chances of leading the project to a successful completion.

## Lesson Objectives

In this lesson, you will:

- Analyze the risks to a project.

- Create a communication plan.

- Plan for change control.

# TOPIC A

# Analyze the Risks to a Project

You are well aware of the potential risks that could affect your project. You now need to analyze them so that they can be mitigated. In this topic, you'll analyze the risks to a project.

The nature of project management has its inherent risks that things can go differently than you had hoped or planned for. Deciding how to approach a project risk early in the planning phase can help you to maximize the opportunities of positive risks and minimize the consequences of adverse risks that may occur during the life of a project.

## Qualitative Analysis

*Qualitative analysis* is a method of assessing, ranking, and prioritizing risks for subsequent analysis. It takes into account the probability of different risks occurring and their likely impact. It is conducted early in the project life cycle so that potential problems can be identified early to develop an effective and favorable outcome. When qualitative analysis is repeated, trends can be evaluated and corrective action may be taken to avoid or lessen a negative consequence.

## Quantitative Analysis

*Quantitative analysis* is a numerical method used to assess the effect of risk and to measure the amount of damage that can take place. Quantifying risk can help you to identify time and cost contingencies of a project and also to prioritize risks. Based on time and budget allotments, the project manager performs quantitative analysis. It involves gathering documents indicating risk planning and project scope, analyzing each risk using risk management tools, and finally taking any alterations into account. Quantitative analysis further refines and enhances the prioritization and scoring produced during qualitative analysis.

## Risk Response Plan

A *risk response plan* is a plan used to decrease the possibility or impact of risk in order to accomplish project objectives. You can create different types of plans to counter risks.

| Risk Response Plan | Used To | Example |
|---|---|---|
| Avoidance | Find a work-around so that the risk never occurs. | Avoid weather damage by doing work indoors. |
| Acceptance | Decide to live with the consequences, should the risk occur. | Cancel the project if funding falls through. |
| Mitigation | Prepare to deal with the risk through contingency planning. | Ask for additional resources to clean up an accidental spill at a worksite that prevents completing tasks. |
| Transference | Get someone else to share the risk or underwrite it for you. | Secure an insurance policy for expensive equipment. |

# Guidelines for Analyzing the Risks to a Project

 **Note:** All Guidelines for this lesson are available as checklists from the **Checklist** tile on the CHOICE Course screen.

Performing risk analysis enables the project team to prioritize risks according to the threat they pose or the opportunity they present to the project. The prioritized list can be used to develop an effective response plan for each risk. Follow these guidelines to analyze the risks to a project.

## Analyze the Risks to a Project

To effectively perform risk analysis, follow these guidelines:

- Examine the list of identified risks and make sure that all the identified risks are documented.
- Include guidelines or requirements regarding the outset of the risk.
- Analyze the data available for each risk.
  - Does the source of the data fully understand the risk?
  - Is the source reliable and trustworthy?
  - Is the amount of data sufficient to adequately analyze the risk?
  - What is the accuracy and quality of the data?
  - Are there risks that require further monitoring?
- Analyze the assumptions identified during risk identification to determine the validity of the assumption and the impact on the project, if false.
- Analyze the probability and impact of each identified risk using well-defined probability and impact scales.
- Consult historical information, such as similar completed projects, studies of similar projects by risk specialists, and risk databases for information that may be useful for risk analysis on your project.
- Prioritize risks.
- Document all changes.

# ACTIVITY 4–1
## Analyzing the Risks to a Project

### Scenario

Previously, you identified the risks to the cooking reality show game application project. Now, you need to analyze those risks so you can plan accordingly should those risks come to impact the project. You complete a Risk Probability and Impact Assessment chart to identify the most important risks and start to create your mitigation plans.

| Risk ID | Risk | Probability | Impact | Risk Score |
|---|---|---|---|---|
| 1 | Steve Jones's Schedule | 5 | 4 | 20 |
| 2 | | | | |
| 3 | | | | |
| 4 | | | | |
| 5 | | | | |

1. Using the provided Risk Probability and Impact Assessment chart, work with your group to fill in some of the project risks and estimate their probability and impact on a scale of 1 to 5 (5 is very high, 1 is very low).

2. In the Risk Probability and Impact Assessment table, fill in the Risk Score for each risk by multiplying the probability by the impact.

3. Which of your risks has the highest Risk Score? What is a possible risk response plan?

# TOPIC B

# Create a Communication Plan

You analyzed risks using different risk analysis methods and planned to mitigate them or reduce their impact on project objectives. Now you may need to ensure that relevant information is available to stakeholders during the course of a project. In this topic, you'll create a communication plan.

An effective communication plan ensures that the right people receive the right information at the right time. You don't want your people expending unnecessary energy reporting on every little detail. Nor do you want to spend hours unnecessarily generating long reports. Mastering the tools and techniques to develop an effective communication management plan will ensure that you deliver the significant information to your stakeholders when they need it.

## Communication Plan

A *communication plan* is a plan that describes what information must be communicated to whom, by whom, when, and in what manner. It is a process of ensuring timely and appropriate collection, generation, storage, dissemination, and ultimate disposition of project information. This plan must be reviewed and updated regularly to ensure it continues to meet the communication needs.

### Example: Communication Planning for Organizing a Conference

Mark has been assigned the responsibility of organizing a conference cosponsored by his company and a few other major companies in the industry. He has to communicate with different people at different levels of management across the various companies. The communication plan may include contact information of the key players in these companies and may stipulate email as the preferred mode of communication.

 **Note:** To learn more about web application vulnerabilities, check out the LearnTO **Plan for Project Communication** presentation from the **LearnTO** tile on the CHOICE Course screen.

## Information Distribution

Information distribution is the process of making information available to the project stakeholders in a timely manner. It not only includes implementation of the communication management plan, but also any unanticipated requests for information.

### Example: Creating Communication Plan to Handle Issues

You are handling a project in which several tasks have been outsourced to another company. There are a lot of communication issues, with team members missing vital project information. You have decided to come up with a communication plan by consulting the stakeholders. You have made final that all documentation be placed on a shared location that all team members can access. Communication between the team members in your company and the employees of the external company should be by email. You also identified members of the external company who will receive status reports and the minutes of the meetings you conduct internally. Additionally, you specify that any requests for project documentation or progress reports outside of the scope of the communication plan will be prioritized and granted via email to the project manager. Finally, you send the communication plan to the stakeholders for their approval.

# Guidelines for Creating a Communication Plan

Effective communication management plans ensure that all project team members are aware of the type and format of information to be shared with project stakeholders. Follow these guidelines to create a communication plan.

## Create a Communication Plan

To create an effective communication management plan, follow these guidelines:

- Determine a collection and filing structure that describes the methods the project team will use to collect and file project information.
- Determine the communication needs of project stakeholders. As a rule of thumb, project team members require more detail on a more frequent basis. Senior management typically requires summary information on a less frequent basis.
  - Work from an organization chart to avoid omitting a key stakeholder.
  - Ask for your project sponsor's input.
  - Ask open-ended questions.
- Analyze the value of providing the information to the project.
- Evaluate any constraints and assumptions to determine their possible impact on communication planning.
- Determine the appropriate communication technologies to use for communicating project information.
  - Determine the immediacy of the need for information.
  - Analyze the availability of technology systems.
  - Evaluate the expected project staff to identify their knowledge of and access to proposed technology.
  - Conduct research to determine the likelihood that there will be changes to the proposed technology before the project is over.
- Determine a distribution structure describing to whom and by whom project information, such as status reports, data schedules, meeting minutes, and so on, should be provided.
- Arrive at schedules for the production of each type of communication.
- Determine methods for accessing information between scheduled communications.
- Specify a method for updating and refining the communication management plan throughout the project life cycle.
- Integrate the communication management plan into the overall project plan.
- Distribute the plan to project stakeholders.

# ACTIVITY 4–2
## Creating a Communication Management Plan

### Data File

C:\095015Data\Planning for Project Risks Communication and Change Management
\communication_plan.docx

### Scenario

You have assembled your team for the cooking reality show game application project. While most of your team is local, several key members are geographically dispersed. The visual design team wants to hold weekly meetings. Also, because of the interdependencies and high risks, you think it would be a good idea to have a daily leads meeting to bring up any issues. You now need to define how your project team will communicate with each other.

1.  Open the **Communication_Plan.docx** file.

2.  On the second line of the communications plan, fill in the Medium and Owner columns. Keep in mind that the team is not working in one place.

3.  Who is the audience for the Monthly Status Meetings? Fill in the Audience column for the Monthly Status Meeting row.

4.  In the first empty row, enter the information for the Visual Design Team Meetings. Use the Technical Design Meetings row as a guideline.

5.  In the last empty row, enter the information for the Daily Leads Meetings.

# TOPIC C

# Plan for Change Control

Now that you have planned the communication, you also need to plan for the changes in your project so that you can minimize any negative impact. In this topic, you will plan for change control.

Change is inevitable and unavoidable in any project. But, you need to make sure that none of the customers, stakeholders, or members of the project management team are surprised by delays to your scope and schedule, or by significant cost overruns. By developing a change control process for your project, documenting its parameters, and adhering to its guidelines, you can move ahead positively.

## Need for Change Control

*Change control* is the process of identifying, documenting, approving or rejecting, and controlling changes to the project baselines. It reduces risks to your project by governing the execution of proposed changes that will affect scope, schedule, cost, and quality. It also allows project managers to record the changes that are requested, make sure that changes are implemented in a standardized and approved manner, minimize their disruptive effect, and monitor their progression from initial request through completion.

> **Note:** There may already be an approved change control process in your organization, in which case it is your responsibility to implement it for your project. If not, it is your responsibility to develop one for your project.

### Example: Change Control Planning for a Conference Project

Ted is a project manager for a large international conference. He has identified that there are too many decision makers on the project, which could be hazardous. Change of key speakers and topics of discussion could have a serious impact on the success of the project. He wants to carry out the changes to the project in a methodical manner, and so he decides to create a change control plan. He begins by gathering relevant information and documentation. He then proceeds to identify the key players within the team who can initiate change requests. He also identifies key stakeholders who will have the authority to approve the change requests. Finally, he documents all the information.

## Guidelines for Planning for Change Control

By developing a change control plan, documenting its parameters, and adhering to its guidelines, you can reduce the risk to your project and maintain its momentum. Follow these guidelines to plan for change control.

### Plan for Change Control

To develop a change control plan, follow these guidelines:

*   Identify what will be considered a change that is significant enough to require management approval. For the sake of maintaining forward momentum on project work, project managers will not bring minor changes to schedule and cost estimates to the top management for approval.
*   Gather any relevant historical data within the organization that relates to the process of identifying, documenting, approving or rejecting, and controlling changes to the project baselines.
*   Determine the latitude the team will have in making autonomous decisions about changes.

- In conversation with stakeholders and the project management team, identify these responsible parties:
    - The people who are able to initiate change requests. These may include stakeholders, project management team members, and customers, among others.
    - The parties who are authorized to give or withhold business approval to a request for a change. Who will make the decision about whether or not a change is necessary and appropriate?
    - The people who have the authority to approve additional funding, overtime costs, purchase orders, and so on.
    - The parties who will be responsible for executing the work necessary to satisfy the requested change, as well as evaluating the work for quality assurance.
    - The person(s) who will be responsible for managing changes. In some organizations, this may be the project manager, but in other organizations, it may be one or more functional managers.
    - The parties who are responsible for prioritizing changes and making qualitative decisions about them. Is this change imperative to the success of the project, or merely nice to have if time and resources allow?
- Identify how change requests must be approved. Some organizations might require written approval from customers before changes to the scope, schedule baseline, and budget can be implemented.
- Make sure that the organizational expectations regarding change control have been clearly defined and documented.

# ACTIVITY 4–3
## Developing a Change Control Plan

### Scenario

Develetech has signed a contract with the television network to deliver the cooking reality show game application project in tandem with the start of the new television season. Therefore, the project has a very tight deadline, as well as a strict budget. You are concerned that any possible changes could negatively affect project performance baselines. You need to ensure that there is a standardized method for handling changes to the project work.

1. **Who will you involve in the change control planning for the project?**
   - ○ Steve Jones
   - ○ Key stakeholders
   - ○ Team members
   - ○ Implementation team members

2. **True or False? Only team members are authorized to initiate a change request.**
   - ☐ True
   - ☐ False

3. **Who would make the decision about whether or not a change is necessary?**
   - ○ Stakeholders
   - ○ Stakeholders and the project team
   - ○ Core team members
   - ○ The project team

4. **True or False? Changes in a project do not usually affect the quality of the project.**
   - ☐ True
   - ☐ False

# Summary

In this lesson, you planned for project risks, communication, and change control. This will help you ensure that your project is conducted with the appropriate internal integrity and oversight.

**How would a project benefit from comprehensive risk planning?**


**Is the change control process in your organization effective? How? If not, how can it be improved?**


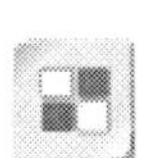 **Note:** Check your CHOICE Course screen for opportunities to interact with your classmates, peers, and the larger CHOICE online community about the topics covered in this course or other topics you are interested in. From the Course screen you can also access available resources for a more continuous learning experience.

# 5 | Managing a Project

**Lesson Time: 1 hour, 30 minutes**

## Lesson Introduction

You finished your project planning and integrated the outputs from each of the planning processes into a comprehensive project management plan. Now you may want to transition your project from planning to execution. In this lesson, you will execute a project plan.

The project team members need a coach to guide them as they undertake the work defined in the scope statement. Executing a project plan ensures that your team is on the same page and that the project is completed on time, within budget, and with the required quality.

## Lesson Objectives

In this lesson, you will:

- Begin project work.

- Execute project plan.

- Track project progress.

- Report performance.

- Implement change control.

# TOPIC A

# Begin Project Work

Your project has officially advanced from the planning stage to execution. Now it's finally time to get started with project work. In this topic, you will begin project work.

All the planning for the project work is done. But, unless you get people to work, you may not be able to meet the project objectives. By bringing all of your team members together and giving them an insight into the goal of the project, you can successfully embark on your project.

## The Team Acquisition Process

The team acquisition process involves identifying team members based on the skills matrix and computing associated costs based on the competencies of each of them. The project manager acquires the resources for the project. During acquisition, the project manager may have to negotiate with the functional manager for the appropriate resources needed for the project. Resources are often pooled within the organization, but they can also be acquired from outside sources with the help of the human resources team or consultants. Cost is the primary criteria when a team member is contracted from outside.

## Kick-Off Meetings

A *kick-off meeting* is conducted by the project manager at the beginning of a project. The meeting is attended by the stakeholders of the project. It is designed to herald the opening of the project work, share information about its importance, articulate project scope, clarify individual as well as project objectives, generate excitement about the work at hand, and secure the enthusiastic participation of all the players. Kick-off meetings are generally held for all projects, but it is recommended for large projects, projects involving new processes or tools, or projects involving new contributors or newly formed teams.

### Example: Kick-Off Meeting For a Training Manual Project

A project on the preparation of a training manual has moved from planning to execution. Naomi, the project manager, has invited all the stakeholders, sponsors, and the team members to a kick-off meeting. She asks someone on the team to take care of the minutes of the meeting, and Bill volunteers to do it. During the meeting, the team discusses the work to be done on the project and the responsibilities of each team member. The team decides to meet every Friday to review the work accomplished in the week and assess the progress of the project. If problems are identified, the team will analyze them and update the plan accordingly.

## Guidelines for Beginning Project Work

 **Note:** All Guidelines for this lesson are available as checklists from the **Checklist** tile on the CHOICE Course screen.

By acquiring a project team and ensuring that all the team members understand the project goals and objectives, you can increase the probability of achieving the project's objectives. Follow these guidelines to begin project work.

### Begin Project Work

To effectively begin the project work, follow these guidelines:

* Conduct a kick-off meeting.

- Call for one team member to take the responsibility of taking notes on important project-specific information.
- Make sure that all team members and sponsors unanimously understand the project charter.
- Review the project plan with contributors.
- Define roles and responsibilities.
- Outline the resources that will be available to the team.
- Have the project sponsor explain why the project's work is important and how its goals are aligned with the larger organizational objectives.
- Document all the decisions and follow-up actions decided in the kick-off meeting.
- Discuss the organizational policies and procedures that the organization has in place regarding project execution to ensure predictable and consistent results. Make sure that all contractors are familiar with the procedures and comply with them.
- In line with good project management practice, use the artifacts necessary to get the job done. Use the organization's project management infrastructure. If it is not there already, then invent it.
- Be vigilant in collecting project information from stakeholders and sponsors.

# ACTIVITY 5–1
## Beginning Project Work

### Scenario

You are now ready to begin work on the cooking reality show game application project. You decide to hold a kickoff meeting. Although celebrity chef, Steve Jones, is not present, the other stakeholders and team members are in attendance. Follow the instructor's lead and participate in the meeting.

---

1. Identify the project manager. The project manager introduces the key players in the project.


2. The project manager asks the project sponsor to give an overview of the project objectives.


3. The project manager asks the team to ask questions and allows anyone to answer as appropriate.

---

# TOPIC B

# Execute the Project Plan

You have acquired your project team and have conducted a project kick-off meeting. It is now finally time to start leveraging the plan. In this topic, you will execute the project plan.

Coordinating people and other resources to carry out the project plan is like conducting an orchestra. Effectively directing and managing project execution ensures that the project team starts and finishes the project work according to the project management plan.

## The Project Execution Process Group

The project execution process group involves carrying out the project plan to produce a product or provide a service. It requires the project team to build on the foundation laid during project plan development. The project manager coordinates, directs, and monitors the progress of the project. This is not just one coherent task, but is a lengthy and complex iterative process.

### Example: Execution of a Research Project

You are the project manager for a research project. A project plan is ready and the project team has begun the work on time. You circulated emails on the organization's policies and procedures and the compliance requirements of the client that the project team needs to adhere to. You decide to meet with the team twice a week to discuss the status of the project and review outstanding issues, if any.

## Quality Assurance

*Quality Assurance (QA)* is a method of evaluating overall project performance through planned, systematic activities; it creates confidence that the project will adhere to the appropriate processes and satisfy standards for quality. It is a part of a continuum of quality activities that begin in the initiating and planning processes and continue throughout the project. It is iterative and it may be adapted based on the identification and resolution of quality problems over the project's life cycle. The quality assurance process varies with the needs of each project.

## Guidelines for Executing the Project Plan

Throughout the entire execution of a project, the project manager can employ various techniques to coordinate and direct the various technical and organizational aspects of the project. Implementing these techniques throughout the project execution will ensure the success of the project. Follow these guidelines to execute a project plan.

### Execute the Project Plan

To effectively execute the project plan, follow these guidelines:

- Ensure that the project starts and finishes on time, within the budget, and within scope.
- Comply with any organizational policies and procedures that the organization has in place regarding project execution to ensure predictable and consistent results. Make sure that all contractors are familiar with and comply with the procedures.
- Decide on a system that will allow you to formally sanction work to commence on an activity or deliverable. The value of the control that your system provides should be balanced with the cost (money and time) of designing, implementing, and using the system.
- Praise and motivate the contributors.
  - Advertise their success. Send out congratulatory email announcements to the whole group when individual contributors make their deadlines or meet the project's requirements.

- Thank contributors for their efforts, both on an individual basis and publicly, during meetings. Note that if you are singling people out for praise, make sure you include everyone who has contributed to avoid inadvertently hurting anyone's feelings.
- Plan and conduct regularly scheduled status review meetings to exchange information concerning the status of work, change requests, and preventive and corrective action:
  - Before the meeting, send a list of open tasks to all participants, so that they can prepare to discuss task status.
  - During the meeting, address each task on the task list by asking the person responsible for the task to report on whether the task has begun, if it has been completed, and how much labor has been spent on it.
  - If problems are identified during a status review meeting, assign them as actions to a responsible person, making sure to include a deadline for resolution. List them on the issues log to be reviewed at a later meeting.
  - Review all outstanding issues. Work through the issues log to check the progress of all the issues listed as outstanding from previous meetings. If necessary, assign additional resources.
  - To encourage participation and commitment, avoid making project status meetings into group disciplinary proceedings. If you feel that an individual team member is not performing adequately, schedule a private meeting with the person to review the matter later.

# ACTIVITY 5-2
## Executing the Project Plan

## Scenario

It is a Monday afternoon at Develetech and your team has gathered for a regular project meeting. Everyone is surprised to find a cake and a cooler with sodas in the room. You announce that this meeting celebrates the official transition of the project from planning to execution. After everyone has had a chance to sample the cake, you settle down to business and review the project schedule.

1. **True or False? The team should work on whatever tasks they want to regardless of the project plan.**
   - ☐ True
   - ☐ False

2. **True or False? Conducting weekly team meetings helps in ensuring that the project schedule completion dates are met.**
   - ☐ True
   - ☐ False

3. **Your team needs to design and develop a game that is fun and represents the Steve Jones show. What should you do to help them meet their objectives?**
   - ○ Command them to come to work on time.
   - ○ Teach them to cook.
   - ○ Monitor their general work performance and keep an eye on how well they adhere to company policies.
   - ○ Make sure they design it the way you would do it.

# TOPIC C

# Track Project Progress

You project is now well into execution. You now need to track the performance of the project progress so that you can be sure that your project is heading in the right direction. In this topic, you will track project performance.

You want to be able to monitor the progress of your project from its initial kick-off through completion so that you can ensure that your project will be delivered on time, on specification, and within the budget. By tracking the contributors' progress against the schedule, identifying common performance problems and red flags that may indicate problems, and negotiating solutions as necessary, you will be able to bring about a successful result.

## Earned Value Analysis

*Earned value analysis* is a method of measuring the performance of a project. It analyzes the project progress by comparing actual schedule and cost performance against planned performance as laid out in the cost and schedule baselines. By this method, you can identify whether the project is on time and within budget.

## Earned Value Calculations

Earned value calculations help you determine if project work is happening as per the plan. There are several terms involved in earned value calculations.

| Term | Description |
| --- | --- |
| *Budget At Completion (BAC)* | The total sum of the budget for a project. |
| *Planned Value (PV)* | The budgeted cost to be spent on a task within a period of time. |
| *Actual Cost (AC)* | The total cost incurred in accomplishing a task within a period of time. |
| *Earned Value (EV)* | The value of work actually accomplished. It is calculated by multiplying the percentage of work completed by the Budget At Completion (BAC). |

**Note:** To learn more about web application vulnerabilities, check out the LearnTO **Analyze Earned Value** presentation from the **LearnTO** tile on the CHOICE Course screen.

## Variance Identification

Variance identification is the process of measuring the differences between the actual project performance and the planned performance. The most commonly used variance measures are cost variance and schedule variance.

| Variance Measure | Description |
| --- | --- |
| *Schedule Variance (SV)* | The difference between the work actually performed and the work scheduled. The formula to find out the schedule variance is SV = EV – PV. A positive variance indicates that your project is ahead of plan, and a negative variance indicates that it is progressing behind schedule. |
| *Cost Variance (CV)* | The difference between the earned value and the actual cost incurred. This will help you to find out whether the project is exceeding or falling within its estimated cost. Cost variance can be calculated by using this formula CV = EV – AC. A positive variance indicates that your project is under spending, and a negative variance indicates that it is over spending. |

## Performance Indices

Performance indices are used to measure the progress of a project toward its set goals.

| Performance Index | Description |
| --- | --- |
| *Cost Performance Index (CPI)* | A measurement of cost efficiency that can be used to determine whether the project is over or under budget. To calculate CPI, you need to divide the earned value (EV) by the actual cost (AC). |
| *Schedule Performance Index (SPI)* | The ratio of work performed to work scheduled. To calculate the SPI, you need to divide the EV by the PV. |

## Variance Management

Variance management is a method of measuring the variances and taking corrective actions in order to achieve the planned outcome. The first step in variance management is performing a root cause analysis at each task level to find out what led to the fall. Once it is identified, the root problem should be worked upon based on real world knowledge and its effect on the project as a whole. When the ideal work around is identified, you need to present the information to the stakeholders to decide if it can be applied.

## Forecasting Techniques

Forecasting techniques are used to determine the expected costs needed to complete project work or an activity in its entirety.

| Forecasting Technique | Description |
| --- | --- |
| *Estimate To Complete (ETC)* | Helps to find how much more it is going to cost to complete the project. It can be calculated by using these formulas:<br>• ETC = (BAC – EV): This formula is used when the current variance is not expected to continue in the future.<br>• ETC = (BAC – EV) / CPI: This can be used when the current variances are seen as typical of future variances. |
| *Estimate At Completion (EAC)* | Represents the projected final costs of work when completed. It can be calculated using this formula: EAC = ETC + AC. |
| *Variance At Completion (VAC)* | The difference between estimate at completion (EAC) and budget at completion (BAC). |

# Guidelines for Tracking Project Progress

Effectively tracking project progress ensures successful project outcome. Follow these guidelines to track project progress.

## Track Project Progress

To effectively track project progress, follow these guidelines:

- Analyze work results against planned performance based on performance elements defined during the planning processes.
  - Involve the team members who are closest to the work in the data analysis. They are the people who understand the work and can probably identify appropriate corrective actions for resolving variances.
  - Use Earned Value techniques to assess cost and schedule progress against planned performance.
  - Evaluate the results of corrective actions to determine whether they have produced the desired results.
- Analyze the results of performance measurements by asking these questions:
  - Is there a variance?
  - What is the cause of the variance?
  - What is the magnitude of the variance? Is the activity causing the variance on the critical path?
  - Is it likely that the variance can be made up in the near future without corrective action or is corrective action necessary to bring the schedule performance back in line with the baseline?
- Hold performance reviews to communicate and assess project status and progress.
- Identify and document corrective action to take to bring expected future project performance in line with planned performance. Depending on the priorities of your project, consider one or more of the following alternatives:
  - Fast-tracking—Perform project activities that have originally been scheduled sequentially and concurrently.
  - Crashing—Allocate more resources to activities so that the project can be completed in less time.
  - Outsourcing—Secure services and expertise from an outside source on a contract or short-term basis.
  - Resource leveling—Readjust the work as appropriate so that people are not overly allocated.
  - Reducing project scope.
- Measure and monitor performance the same way throughout the project life cycle so that meaningful comparisons can be made.
- Document lessons learned during schedule control for use in future projects. The documentation should include:
  - Causes of variances.
  - Performance baselines affected by the changes and rationale behind the recommended corrective action.
  - Any other lessons learned during schedule control.

# ACTIVITY 5–3
## Calculating Earned Value

## Scenario

You are well into executing your project at Develetech for developing the Steve Jones cooking show game. Your team has presented you with the following status data for the "Develop Storyboard" work package:

- Planned Value (PV) = $7,500
- Percent of Work Complete = 40%
- Actual Cost (AC) = $2,500
- Number of days scheduled = 30
- Actual number of days completed = 20

---

1. **What is the earned value for this work package?**
   - ○ $7,500
   - ○ $5,000
   - ○ $3,000
   - ○ $2,500

2. **Calculate planned value for the "Develop Storyboard" work package for the actual number of days.**
   - ○ $2,500
   - ○ $500
   - ○ $4,500
   - ○ $5,000

3. **What is the cost variance for the work package?**
   - ○ $3,000
   - ○ $2,500
   - ○ $1,000
   - ○ $500

4. **What does the cost variance indicate?**
   - ○ The project is over budget by $500.
   - ○ The project is under budget by $500.
   - ○ The project is over budget by $2,500.
   - ○ The project is under budget by $2,500.

5. **What formula would you use to calculate SPI?**
   - ○ EV – PV
   - ○ EV / PV
   - ○ EV – AC
   - ○ EV / AC

6. Calculate the CPI for the project.
   - ○ 1.4
   - ○ 0.1
   - ○ 1.2
   - ○ 0.2

7. What does the Cost Performance Index (CPI) of 1.2 for the project indicate?
   - ○ The project is performing under budget.
   - ○ The project is performing over budget.
   - ○ The project is within budget.
   - ○ The project is behind schedule and is over budget.

8. True or False? SPI of 1.0 means the project is right on schedule.
   - ☐ True
   - ☐ False

9. Identify a benefit of conducting the earned value analysis.
   - ○ It provides a more accurate project baseline than other tracking methods.
   - ○ It allows you to track project performance and also acts as a means to forecast project performance.
   - ○ Management can understand earned value analysis better than other measures.
   - ○ Helps identify what the project team has accomplished so far.

10. Your team has been working well ever since the project started. But, over the past couple of weeks, you have observed a dip in performance. What steps can you take to help the team perform better? (Choose two.)
    - ☐ During team meetings, shower praise on members who performed well and condemn the non-performers.
    - ☐ Tighten the deadlines to improve productivity.
    - ☐ Encourage team members to share their experiences with others.
    - ☐ Appreciate good efforts during team meetings and organize events for recognizing team members who have performed well.

# TOPIC D

# Report Performance

You have tracked the progress of a project. Now you would like to keep the stakeholders informed about the current status of the project. In this topic, you will report project performance.

As a project manager, you need to communicate project performance to the top management, stakeholders, and customers, and reassure them that the work is on time and within budget. Effective performance reporting enables you—as well as your team members, sponsors, stakeholders, and customers—to make reasoned, informed, and timely decisions regarding projects.

## Performance Reporting

*Performance reporting* is the process of gathering and communicating information regarding the current status of a project as well as projections for progress over time. During performance reporting, information regarding the work being accomplished and resources being used is collected, analyzed, and displayed in various report formats. The performance reports help to compare the current execution status of the project with the originally approved plans and identify deviations. They also serve as historical information that may be used in future projects.

## Types of Performance Reports

There are three types of performance reports: status reports, progress reports, and forecast reports.

| Report Type | Description |
| --- | --- |
| Status report | Describes what has been achieved in the current period; what is the current status of the budget, scope, and schedules; what issues, risks, and variances have been identified and how to correct them; and what has been planned for the next period. |
| Progress report | Gives a summary of the progress of the project towards its objectives, provides historical progress information of the project from its initiation, and compares the progress made so far to the progress that was originally expected. |
| Forecast report | Projects the timelines and cost of a project for a future period based on the current status of the project. |

## Example: Status Report for a Construction Project

Eric is the project manager of a construction project. He has to present reports on the project's performance to the stakeholders. He consolidates the information on variances from the agreed baselines as per the guidelines and procedures laid down in the project plan. Eric creates a status report detailing the accomplishments in the current reporting period, highlighting the current status of the costs, scope, and schedules. The team had to deal with unexpected increases in steel prices in the current period. Eric presents this as the reason behind the huge cost variances. Though there has been a sharp increase in costs, the project team has identified areas where cost reduction methods can be applied. Eric will present this information to the stakeholders while explaining how the project will progress further.

**Note:** To learn more about web application vulnerabilities, check out the LearnTO **Report on Project Status** presentation from the **LearnTO** tile on the CHOICE Course screen.

## Personnel Evaluations

Personnel evaluations involve tracking the performance of team members and providing feedback. The project manager needs to perform formal or informal assessments of team members throughout a project's life cycle to manage conflicts, resolve issues, and appraise the performance of individual team members. Personnel evaluations help managers to identify whether the team members require training and to organize training on technical or soft skills as required. It also enables project managers to plan for recognition events to motivate the team, and improve the team's competencies and attitudes to help them perform better.

## Guidelines for Reporting Performance

Communicating information using performance reports helps the team pinpoint problems that may need to be resolved. It also enhances the team's ability to implement corrective actions early enough to make a positive difference to the end result of a project. Follow these guidelines to report performance.

### Report Performance

To effectively report project performance, follow these guidelines:

- Consult your project plan's subsidiary plans for guidelines and procedures for reporting on the various aspects of project performance.
- Determine the type of report needed for the information being reported. Make sure that the format of the report adequately provides the type of information and level of detail required by various stakeholders.
- Prepare performance reports that provide the required information in a format that enhances understanding of the material. Formal reports should contain:
  - A cover page with the project name, project manager's name, type of report, and date of report.
  - A description of the project's actual accomplishments for the reporting period as compared to the goals established for the period. In addition, any changes implemented or anticipated should be described.
  - Interim performance reports should include a forecast of how the project is expected to perform in the future.
  - End of project reports should include a brief description of major accomplishments, an evaluation of the project's performance, an explanation of any variances in the performance and project objectives, and any future plans for the project.
  - Appendices, which may include any supporting material that contributes to an understanding of the project and its progress to date, such as charts, tables, and samples.
- Balance the cost, time, and logistics of preparing performance reports against the benefits gained by the reporting.

# ACTIVITY 5–4
## Reporting Project Performance

### Scenario

As the project manager of the game application project, you have to inform the stakeholders about the current status of the project and explain whether the project will meet its objectives. Though you have calculated variances, it is important to present them in a format that will help the stakeholders understand how the project is progressing and foresee its position in the future.

1. **What information does a status report convey to the stakeholders?**
   - ○ The exemplary performance of one of the assistant chefs.
   - ○ A prediction of the final cost the project will incur.
   - ○ A description of the project costs and schedules for the current reporting period.
   - ○ The conflicts between the team members and how the project manager resolved them.

2. **What is a benefit of a project forecast report to the project team and the senior management?**
   - ○ Pinpoints the problem areas of the project.
   - ○ Identifies where the project will stand if it progresses at the current rate.
   - ○ Identifies the team members responsible for the projected success or failure of the project.
   - ○ Analyzes the status of the project as against original plans.

3. **True or False? Personnel evaluations help to identify the training requirements of a project team.**
   - ☐ True
   - ☐ False

# TOPIC E

# Implement Change Control

Now that you have executed the project plan and have taken steps to make sure that your project is conducted with appropriate integrity and oversight, you will go further by controlling the changes to the project work, budget, and schedule baseline. In this topic, you will implement the change control plan.

Sometimes you may have to make sure that none of the customers, stakeholders, or members of the project management team are surprised by a sudden change in scope, delays to your schedule, or significant cost overruns. By controlling the changes in your project, documenting its parameters, and adhering to the change control guidelines, you can reduce the risk to your project and maintain its positive forward movement.

## Elements of a Change Request

Change requests are formal documents, letters, memos, or even meeting minutes, that describe a request for change and the implications of the change to the project. They contain certain basic elements of information.

| Element | Description |
| --- | --- |
| Change | Describe the change requested. Include specific criteria that can be used to measure the change. |
| Requested By | Who is requesting the change. |
| Reason for Change | Why the change is being made; how the change will benefit the outcome of the project. |
| Method of Change | How the change will be implemented. |
| Affected Parties | Who will be affected by the change. |
| Affect on Success Criteria | How will the change affect:<br>• Scope<br>• Time<br>• Cost<br>• Quality |
| Backup Information | Any additional information that is needed to support or explain the nature of the change. |
| Sign-offs | Who approved the change. |
| Date of Approval | When was the change approved. |

 **Access the Checklist tile on your CHOICE Course screen for reference information and job aids on How to Implement Change Control.**

# ACTIVITY 5-5
# Implementing Change Control

## Scenario

As you continue managing the execution of the Steve Jones game application project, you become aware of some requested changes that could negatively affect project performance baselines. You need to ensure that the changes do not affect project work, budget, and schedule baseline. Use the following table as a guideline to implement a change request.

| Change Request Field | Your Entry |
| --- | --- |
| Change | |
| Requested By | |
| Reason for Change | |
| Method of Change | |
| Affected Parties | |
| Affect on Success Criteria | |
| Backup Information | |
| Sign-offs | |
| Date of Approval | |

1. Steve Jones has recently become enamored with virtual reality. He is now insisting that the game be implemented in a full 3D immersive experience. Enter as much information as you can into the change request.

2. Based on the information in the change request, what action should you take? (Choose two.)
   - ☐ Bring information to all the team members for evaluation.
   - ☐ Coordinate changes across knowledge areas.
   - ☐ Identify corrective action to be taken to resolve the problem.
   - ☐ Bring information to all the key stakeholders.
   - ☐ Update the project plan to reflect changes.

3. Who will you involve in the change control process for the project?
   - ○ People involved in the project.
   - ○ All the team members.
   - ○ Key stakeholders.
   - ○ Implementation team members.

4. True or False? Change requests should be justified before analysis.
   - ☐ True
   - ☐ False

# Summary

In this lesson, you managed project execution. Executing a job according to the project plan ensures that your team is on the same page and that your project finishes on time, within budget, and with the required quality.

**In your experience, what aspects of executing the project plan have you found to be the most challenging? Why?**

**What analysis techniques would you use to execute future projects effectively?**

 **Note:** Check your CHOICE Course screen for opportunities to interact with your classmates, peers, and the larger CHOICE online community about the topics covered in this course or other topics you are interested in. From the Course screen you can also access available resources for a more continuous learning experience.

# 6 | Closing the Project

**Lesson Time: 30 minutes**

## Lesson Introduction

You have successfully executed the project plan and obtained all deliverables from the project team. You are ready to hand over the project to the customer. In this lesson, you will close the project.

Unfinished business, contracts not correctly closed out, and poor documentation can turn into months of additional work and expenditures. The last thing you do on a project will be the first thing people remember about your efforts overall. Formal project closure helps ensure that there are no loose ends that could unravel the good work of your team and the success of your project.

## Lesson Objectives

In this lesson, you will:

- Close a project.

- Create a final report.

# TOPIC A

# Close a Project

You implemented the project plan and executed all project activities. It is time now to bring the project to a formal conclusion and hand over the deliverables to the stakeholders. In this topic, you will close out a project.

Ending a project requires the same care and attention as starting a project. It is necessary to ensure that stakeholders are satisfied with the project's outcome. Obtaining the stakeholders' formal acceptance of your project's outcome ensures that the project is properly closed.

## Closeout Elements

Closing a project involves many elements that are documented and archived.

| Element | Description |
| --- | --- |
| Project Outcome | The final product, service, or result that the project was expected to produce. |
| Project Files | A collection of all the documents produced during the course of the project. |
| Formal Acceptance Documentation | Documentation that confirms that the stakeholders have formally accepted that the project has met the requirements and that the deliverables satisfy the specifications. |
| Project Closure Documents | Formal documentation indicating project completion. If the project was terminated before completion, this documentation specifies the reasons for the termination. |
| Historical Information | Lessons learned and other information to be archived for future reference. |
| Contract Documentation | Documents containing the contract information of the resources. |
| Reports | Project performance reports, performance evaluation reports, and any other reports generated throughout the project. |

## The Project Closeout Process

The *project closeout* process involves closing out all activities and formally ending the project or, in the case of multiphase projects, closing out a specific project phase. It coordinates activities needed to verify and document project deliverables, to obtain the stakeholders' acceptance of the deliverables, to confirm that the project has met all requirements, and to identify reasons if a project is terminated before completion. Upon completion of these activities, the process authorizes a formal handoff of project deliverables to the stakeholders. The process also includes other activities to collect project records, analyze project success or failure, archive project information and lessons learned, release resources, and close contracts.

**Access the Checklist tile on your CHOICE Course screen for reference information and job aids on How to Close a Project.**

# ACTIVITY 6–1
## Closing a Project

## Scenario

Your good planning and control has resulted in the cooking reality show game application project coming to a successful close. The final project deliverable is complete. It is now time to hand over the project to the stakeholders and bring it to a formal conclusion.

1. **What is an element of project closeout that requires the stakeholders' acceptance?**
   - ○ Recipes included in the application.
   - ○ Minutes of all project status meetings.
   - ○ The final code and installation packages of the game.
   - ○ Documentation of lessons learned from the project.

2. **What project information is important and needs to be archived for future reference? (Choose two.)**
   - ☐ Audio and video shooting activities for the animations.
   - ☐ The deviations in the project schedules, reasons for the deviations, and steps taken to keep the project on track.
   - ☐ Steve Jones's autograph and photographs with the project team.
   - ☐ Variances between planned cost and actual cost, and steps taken to keep the project as much within budget as possible.

3. **True or False? You need to bring Steve Jones's contract agreement to a formal closure as part of the project closeout process.**
   - ☐ True
   - ☐ False

4. **What activity will you perform as part of the project closeout process?**
   - ○ Collect anecdotes from Steve Jones.
   - ○ Obtain a formal acceptance of the project deliverables from the stakeholders.
   - ○ Shoot pictures of the food cooked while creating video animations.
   - ○ Bring major project issues to the notice of the senior management.

# TOPIC B

# Create a Final Report

You have performed the project closeout operations. Now, you may need to summarize all that happened in the project and make information available to management. In this topic, you will create a final report.

The successful completion of a project does not imply that everything went on smoothly throughout the project's life cycle. There might have been problems with resources, schedule conflicts, or any other issue that the project manager and the team have encountered and tackled successfully. Documenting this information as a final report and presenting it to the stakeholders and senior management will not only bring out the efforts put in or the decisions taken by the project team, but would also help management to make informed decisions while handling similar projects in the future.

## Final Report

The *final report* is a report that summarizes what happened in the project. It is prepared for all projects, irrespective of whether a project has been completed successfully or not. It presents an overview of the project, an evaluation of the team's performance, a list of issues encountered, a summary of what went right and what went wrong, a commentary on the deviations from the original plan and budget, a summary of major accomplishments of the project team, and a record of recommendations for future projects. The final report is made available to senior management, stakeholders, and other project managers to apply the experience in future projects.

### Example: Preparing a Final Report for a Website Project

You are the manager for a project to create a website for your company. Now that you have completed the project, you prepare the final report. In it, you provide an overview of the project's initial objectives and specifications, highlight key changes to the objectives, and explain how the changes were carried out. You also provide comparisons between the planned dates and the actual dates in which deliverables were completed. As part of the evaluation of the project team's performance, you highlight the major accomplishments of the team. After describing all that happened in this project, you also provide recommendations for future similar projects.

## Guidelines for Creating a Final Report

> **Note:** All Guidelines for this lesson are available as checklists from the **Checklist** tile on the CHOICE Course screen.

The final report documents all that happened in a project for future reference. Follow these guidelines for creating a final report.

### Create a Final Report

To create an effective final report, follow these guidelines:

- Make a summary of how the project was carried out.

  - Provide an overview of the project's initial objectives and specifications.
  - Explain any changes to objectives and specifications, the reasons behind the changes, and how the changes were executed.
  - Present the original project plans, list revisions to those plans if any, and provide reasons for the revisions.
  - Present the initial budget, identify the actual project costs, and explain variances if any.

- Describe the deliverables of each phase.
- If the project was terminated prior to completion, state reasons why.
- Evaluate the performance of the project team.
  - Comment on the performance of each individual on the project team.
  - Highlight the major accomplishments of the project team.
  - Comment on the relationship between the project team, the stakeholders, and the senior management.
  - Acknowledge the contributions of the project team.
  - Identify mistakes committed and bring poor performance to notice.
  - Explain any conflicts in the team and how they were resolved.
- Explain the issues encountered.
  - Identify the issues encountered throughout the project's life cycle and explain how they were tackled.
  - List any issues that could not be resolved.
- Provide recommendations for future similar projects.
  - Explain lessons learned in the project and provide suggestions for better performance.
  - Suggest changes in the existing policies and procedures.
  - Bring out new ideas for improving project performance.

# ACTIVITY 6–2
## Creating a Final Report

### Scenario

The stakeholders of the game application project have approved the project's deliverables and you have performed all the activities pertaining to the formal conclusion of the project. Though the project has been completed successfully, you encountered many issues during its life cycle. You would like to document all such information so that it is helpful for project managers handling similar projects in the future.

---

1.  **What information would you include in the final report of the project? (Choose two.)**

    ☐  A list of files and documentation generated during the project's life cycle.

    ☐  Documentation of the contract signed with Steve Jones.

    ☐  The outstanding coordination within the project team that ensured completion of the project on time and within budget.

    ☐  Steve Jones was unable to complete the final audio recording and the audio engineer had to recreate some pieces from pre-recorded words.

2.  **True or False? The final report is presented to the stakeholders, the project team, and the senior management.**

    ☐  True

    ☐  False

3.  **One of the developers was a wonderful worker. She always showed up prepared, worked hard and smart, and was willing to do more than her share of project tasks. However, she skipped or was late for at least 50 percent of the team meetings. What commentary would you include while evaluating her performance in the final report? (Choose three.)**

    ☐  The developer's unwillingness to participate in team meetings made things more difficult for others on the team.

    ☐  She made group decision making harder.

    ☐  She made team communication more complex, and her absence was probably a morale buster.

    ☐  Though she was unwilling to attend the meetings, her work compensated for her behavior.

4.  **What is a valid recommendation for future projects?**

    ○  Hire Steve Jones as the key personality for all future game projects.

    ○  Strive to complete projects ahead of scheduled time by stretching the working time of resources.

    ○  Establish a communication protocol among the project team and stakeholders.

    ○  Compensate on the quality of the product if the cost to the company can be reduced.

---

# Summary

In this lesson, you executed the closeout phase of a project. This enables you to formally hand off the project and deliverables to the stakeholders and bring the project to completion.

**What lessons have you learned from your project? What major issues arose and how were they resolved?**

**What are the major accomplishments of your project team? How would you highlight this information in the final report?**

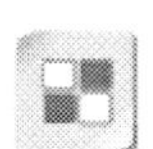

> **Note:** Check your CHOICE Course screen for opportunities to interact with your classmates, peers, and the larger CHOICE online community about the topics covered in this course or other topics you are interested in. From the Course screen you can also access available resources for a more continuous learning experience.

# Course Follow-Up

Congratulations! You have completed the *Project Management Fundamentals (Third Edition)* course. In this course, you examined the elements of sound project management and applied its generally recognized practices to manage projects. You now have the skills and knowledge required to successfully manage projects in your organization.

## What's Next?

To expand on your knowledge of project management concepts, you may wish to take the *CompTIA® Project+ Certification* course as well as *Project Management Professional (PMP) Training: Aligned with PMBOK Guide Fifth Edition*. Also consider improving your business communication skills by taking any of the Workplace Skills courses offered by Logical Operations.

You are encouraged to explore project management fundamentals further by actively participating in any of the social media forums set up by your instructor or training administrator through the **Social Media** tile on the CHOICE Course screen.

# A | Logical Operations Master Mobile Application Developer (MMAD) Exam MAD-111 Objectives

The following table indicates where the Logical Operations Master Mobile Application Developer (MMAD) Exam MAD-111 certification objectives are covered in the Logical Operations *Developing Secure Android™ Apps for Business, Developing Secure iOS® Apps for Business*, and *Project Management Fundamentals (Third Edition)* courses.

| Exam Objective | Course, Lesson, and Topic Reference |
| --- | --- |
| **Domain 1.0 Android Mobile Application Development** | |
| **Objective 1.1 Given a set of requirements and expectations, develop an Android app with multiple activities** | |
| • Android operating system | Android Apps, Topic 1-A |
| • Versions | Android Apps, Topic 1-A |
| • Marshmallow | Android Apps, Topic 1-A |
| • Nougat | Android Apps, Topic 1-A |
| • Version feature | Android Apps, Topic 1-A |
| • Hardware support | Android Apps, Topic 1-A |
| • API levels | Android Apps, Topic 1-A |
| • Android app development tools | Android Apps, Topic 1-B |
| • JDK | Android Apps, Topic 1-B |
| • Android Studio | Android Apps, Topic 1-B |
| • Android SDK | Android Apps, Topic 1-B |
| • Android SDK Manager | Android Apps, Topic 1-B |
| • Command-line tools | Android Apps, Topic 1-B |

| Exam Objective | Course, Lesson, and Topic Reference |
|---|---|
| • Android Virtual Device Manager | Android Apps, Topic 1-B |
| • Emulators | Android Apps, Topic 1-B |
| • Android architecture | Android Apps, Topic 1-A |
| • Kernel | Android Apps, Topic 1-A |
| • Libraries | Android Apps, Topic 1-A |
| • Android Runtime | Android Apps, Topic 1-A |
| • Application framework | Android Apps, Topic 1-A |
| • Applications | Android Apps, Topic 1-A |
| • The Android project structure | Android Apps, Topic 2-A |
| • Manifests | Android Apps, Topic 2-A |
| • Java | Android Apps, Topic 2-A |
| • Res | Android Apps, Topic 2-A |
| • Activities | Android Apps, Topic 2-A |
| • Layouts | Android Apps, Topic 2-A |
| • View groups and objects | Android Apps, Topic 2-A |
| • Intents and bundles | Android Apps, Topic 2-A |
| • Resource files and directories | Android Apps, Topic 2-A |
| • Fragments and multiple activities | Android Apps, Topics 2-A, 2-C, 3-A, 3-B |
| • The app lifecycle | Android Apps, Topic 2-C |
| • App organization | Android Apps, Topic 2-C |
| • Device screens | Android Apps, Topic 2-C |
| • Device and app buttons | Android Apps, Topic 2-C |
| • UI states | Android Apps, Topic 2-C |
| • The activity lifecycle | Android Apps, Topic 2-C |
| • The fragment lifecycle | Android Apps, Topic 2-C |
| • Memory management and multitasking | Android Apps, Topic 2-C |
| • Design requirements and expectations | Android Apps, Topic 2-D |
| • Material design | Android Apps, Topic 2-D |
| • Android user expectations | Android Apps, Topic 2-D |
| • Mobile device constraints | Android Apps, Topic 2-D |
| **Objective 1.2 Implement the use of resources, multimedia assets, data, and storage** | |
| • Resources | Android Apps, Topics 4-A, 4-B |
| • Resource loading | Android Apps, Topic 4-B |
| • Languages | Android Apps, Topic 4-B |
| • Themes and styles | Android Apps, Topic 4-C |

| Exam Objective | Course, Lesson, and Topic Reference |
|---|---|
| • Images | Android Apps, Topic 5-A |
| • Code-generated graphics | Android Apps, Topic 5-B |
| • Animation | Android Apps, Topic 5-C |
| • Data storage | Android Apps, Topics 6-A, 6-B |
| • Data storage preferences | Android Apps, Topic 6-A |
| • Internal storage | Android Apps, Topic 6-A |
| • External storage | Android Apps, Topic 6-A |
| • SQLite | Android Apps, Topic 6-A |
| • Remote storage | Android Apps, Topic 6-A |
| • Write data | Android Apps, Topic 6-A |
| • Read data | Android Apps, Topic 6-B |
| • Web data | Android Apps, Topics 8-A, 8-B |
| • AsyncTask | Android Apps, Topic 8-A |
| • XML data | Android Apps, Topic 8-A |
| • ListView adapter | Android Apps, Topic 8-A |
| • Predefined list layouts | Android Apps, Topic 8-A |
| • WebView | Android Apps, Topic 8-B |
| **Objective 1.3 Perform Android app debugging and analysis tasks** | |
| • Android Debug Bridge | Android Apps, Topic 7-A |
| • Frames | Android Apps, Topic 7-A |
| • Threads | Android Apps, Topic 7-A |
| • Variables | Android Apps, Topic 7-A |
| • Watches | Android Apps, Topic 7-A |
| • Breakpoints | Android Apps, Topic 7-A |
| • LogCat | Android Apps, Topic 7-B |
| • Android Device Monitor | Android Apps, Topic 7-B |
| • DDMS | Android Apps, Topic 7-B |
| • Dev Tool app | Android Apps, Topic 7-B |
| **Objective 1.4 Implement a user preferences screen to enable customization** | |
| • Preferences layout | Android Apps, Topic 9-A |
| • Activity and fragment preferences | Android Apps, Topic 9-A |
| • Preference management | Android Apps, Topic 9-B |
| **Objective 1.5 Integrate app functionality with system resources** | |
| • Alternate layouts | Android Apps, Topic 10-A |

| Exam Objective | Course, Lesson, and Topic Reference |
| --- | --- |
| • Screen size | Android Apps, Topic 10-A |
| • Screen layout | Android Apps, Topic 10-A |
| • Pixel density | Android Apps, Topic 10-A |
| • API versions | Android Apps, Topic 10-A |
| • Sensors | Android Apps, Topic 10-B |
| • Motion | Android Apps, Topic 10-B |
| • Environment | Android Apps, Topic 10-B |
| • Position | Android Apps, Topic 10-B |
| • Sensor framework | Android Apps, Topic 10-B |
| • Location services | Android Apps, Topic 10-B |
| • Multimedia capture | Android Apps, Topic 10-C |
| • Multimedia framework | Android Apps, Topic 10-C |
| • Widgets | Android Apps, Topic 10-D |

**Objective 1.6 Finalize an Android app**

| Exam Objective | Course, Lesson, and Topic Reference |
| --- | --- |
| • Android mobile app security | Android Apps, Topic 11-A |
| • Linux kernel security | Android Apps, Topic 11-A |
| • App isolation | Android Apps, Topic 11-A |
| • APK files | Android Apps, Topic 11-A |
| • Permissions | Android Apps, Topic 11-A |
| • Installation | Android Apps, Topic 11-A |
| • Runtime | Android Apps, Topic 11-A |
| • Encryption/decryption | Android Apps, Topic 11-A |
| • JCA | Android Apps, Topic 11-A |
| • Gradle and manifest preparation | Android Apps, Topic 11-B |
| • Method reference limit | Android Apps, Topic 11-B |
| • ProGuard | Android Apps, Topic 11-B |
| • Digital signatures | Android Apps, Topic 11-B |

**Domain 2.0 iOS Mobile Application Development**

**Objective 2.1 Understand iOS app design standards**

| Exam Objective | Course, Lesson, and Topic Reference |
| --- | --- |
| • Design process phases | iOS Apps, Topic 4-A |
| • Define the concept | iOS Apps, Topic 4-A |
| • Identify the data sources | iOS Apps, Topic 4-A |
| • UI design | iOS Apps, Topic 4-A |
| • Define the interactions | iOS Apps, Topic 4-A |
| • UI standards | iOS Apps, Topic 4-A |

| Exam Objective | Course, Lesson, and Topic Reference |
| --- | --- |
| • iOS user expectations | iOS Apps, Topic 4-A |
| • iOS design patterns | iOS Apps, Topic 4-B |
| • MVC | iOS Apps, Topic 4-B |
| • Target-Action | iOS Apps, Topic 4-B |
| • Delegation | iOS Apps, Topic 4-B |
| **Objective 2.2 Given a set of requirements and expectations, develop an iOS mobile app** | |
| • iOS development tools | iOS Apps, Topic 1-A |
| • Xcode | iOS Apps, Topic 1-A |
| • Features | iOS Apps, Topic 1-A |
| • Preferences | iOS Apps, Topic 1-A |
| • Navigation | iOS Apps, Topic 1-A |
| • The Simulator application | iOS Apps, Topic 1-A |
| • The iOS SDK | iOS Apps, Topic 1-A |
| • Cross-platform tools | iOS Apps, Topic 4-A |
| • Sencha | iOS Apps, Topic 4-A |
| • PhoneGap | iOS Apps, Topic 4-A |
| • Appcelerator Titanium | iOS Apps, Topic 4-A |
| • Qt | iOS Apps, Topic 4-A |
| • Xamarin | iOS Apps, Topic 4-A |
| • Alpha Anywhere | iOS Apps, Topic 4-A |
| • Microsoft Visual Studio | iOS Apps, Topic 4-A |
| • Apple developer program accounts | iOS Apps, Topic 1-A |
| • Swift | iOS Apps, Topics 1-B, 1-C, 1-D |
| • Swift Standard Library | iOS Apps, Topic 1-B |
| • The playground | iOS Apps, Topic 1-B |
| • Comments | iOS Apps, Topic 1-B |
| • Variables | iOS Apps, Topic 1-B |
| • Constants | iOS Apps, Topic 1-C |
| • Data types | iOS Apps, Topic 1-C |
| • Named | iOS Apps, Topic 1-C |
| • Compound | iOS Apps, Topic 1-C |
| • Optional | iOS Apps, Topic 1-C |
| • Custom | iOS Apps, Topic 1-D |
| • Operators | iOS Apps, Topic 1-C |
| • Assignment | iOS Apps, Topic 1-C |

| Exam Objective | Course, Lesson, and Topic Reference |
| --- | --- |
| • Arithmetic | iOS Apps, Topic 1-C |
| • Comparison | iOS Apps, Topic 1-C |
| • Logical | iOS Apps, Topic 1-C |
| • Access levels | iOS Apps, Topic 1-D |
| • Public | iOS Apps, Topic 1-D |
| • Internal | iOS Apps, Topic 1-D |
| • Private | iOS Apps, Topic 1-D |
| • Flow control | iOS Apps, Topic 1-F |
| • iOS frameworks | iOS Apps, Topic 1-B |
| • Core OS | iOS Apps, Topic 1-B |
| • Core Services | iOS Apps, Topic 1-B |
| • Cocoa Touch | iOS Apps, Topic 1-B |
| • Media | iOS Apps, Topic 1-B |
| • iOS app projects | iOS Apps, Topic 2-A |
| • Project templates | iOS Apps, Topic 2-A |
| • UI layouts | iOS Apps, Topic 2-B |
| • Views | iOS Apps, Topics 2-A, 2-B |
| • NIBs and XIBs | iOS Apps, Topic 2-A |
| • The Storyboard Editor | iOS Apps, Topic 2-B |
| • Constraints | iOS Apps, Topic 8-A |
| • View events and user interactions | iOS Apps, Topic 3-A |
| • Actions and outlets | iOS Apps, Topic 3-A |
| **Objective 2.3 Implement multiple view navigation** | |
| • Navigation patterns | iOS Apps, Topic 5-A |
| • Single view | iOS Apps, Topic 5-A |
| • Linear | iOS Apps, Topic 5-A |
| • Hierarchical | iOS Apps, Topic 5-A |
| • Hybrid | iOS Apps, Topic 5-A |
| • Navigation components | iOS Apps, Topic 5-A |
| • Navigation controller | iOS Apps, Topic 5-A |
| • Tab bar controller | iOS Apps, Topic 5-A |
| • Page view controller | iOS Apps, Topic 5-A |
| • Custom classes | iOS Apps, Topic 5-B |
| **Objective 2.4 Implement the use of data, graphics, and media** | |
| • Data storage options | iOS Apps, Topic 6-A |

| Exam Objective | Course, Lesson, and Topic Reference |
| --- | --- |
| • Data storage preferences | iOS Apps, Topic 6-A |
| • Property lists | iOS Apps, Topic 6-A |
| • Embedded resources and files | iOS Apps, Topic 6-A |
| • Local app files | iOS Apps, Topic 6-A |
| • JSON | iOS Apps, Topic 6-A |
| • SQLite | iOS Apps, Topic 6-A |
| • Core Data | iOS Apps, Topic 6-A |
| • Web services | iOS Apps, Topic 6-A |
| • Cloud storage | iOS Apps, Topic 6-A |
| • Keychain services | iOS Apps, Topic 6-A |
| • The iOS file system | iOS Apps, Topic 6-A |
| • Table view | iOS Apps, Topic 6-B |
| • Preferences view | iOS Apps, Topic 6-D |
| • Segues | iOS Apps, Topics 2-B, 6-B |
| • OpenURL | iOS Apps, Topic 6-C |
| • UIImage view | iOS Apps, Topic 7-A |
| • Core Graphics | iOS Apps, Topic 7-B |
| • UIView Drawing model | iOS Apps, Topic 7-B |
| • iOS Animation | iOS Apps, Topic 7-C |
| • Core Animation | iOS Apps, Topic 7-C |
| **Objective 2.5 Integrate app functionality with system resources** | |
| • App states | iOS Apps, Topic 8-A |
| • Background state | iOS Apps, Topic 8-A |
| • State change methods | iOS Apps, Topic 8-A |
| • View controller methods | iOS Apps, Topic 8-A |
| • Stack view | iOS Apps, Topic 8-A |
| • On-screen keyboard | iOS Apps, Topic 8-A |
| • Queued notifications | iOS Apps, Topic 8-A |
| • Capabilities | iOS Apps, Topic 8-B |
| • In-app purchase | iOS Apps, Topic 8-B |
| • Push notifications | iOS Apps, Topic 8-B |
| • Maps | iOS Apps, Topic 8-B |
| • Map Kit Framework | iOS Apps, Topic 8-B |
| • Core Location | iOS Apps, Topic 8-B |
| **Objective 2.6 Perform debugging and maintenance tasks** | |

| Exam Objective | Course, Lesson, and Topic Reference |
| --- | --- |
| • Xcode debugging features | iOS Apps, Topics 1-A, 1-B, 9-A |
| • Errors | iOS Apps, Topic 9-B |
| • Simple domain | iOS Apps, Topic 9-B |
| • Recoverable | iOS Apps, Topic 9-B |
| • Logic failure | iOS Apps, Topic 9-B |
| • Universal | iOS Apps, Topic 9-B |
| • Error reporting and handling | iOS Apps, Topic 9-B |
| • Alerts | iOS Apps, Topic 9-B |
| **Objective 2.7 Finalize an iOS app** | |
| • iOS security architecture | iOS Apps, Topic 9-C |
| • Software | iOS Apps, Topic 9-C |
| • Hardware and firmware | iOS Apps, Topic 9-C |
| • iOS security features | iOS Apps, Topic 9-C |
| • Secure boot chain | iOS Apps, Topic 9-C |
| • System software authorization | iOS Apps, Topic 9-C |
| • Secure enclave | iOS Apps, Topic 9-C |
| • Touch ID | iOS Apps, Topic 9-C |
| • Encryption | iOS Apps, Topic 9-C |
| • File data protection | iOS Apps, Topic 9-C |
| • Network security | iOS Apps, Topic 9-C |
| • App Store review | iOS Apps, Topic 9-C |
| • The iOS Keychain API | iOS Apps, Topic 9-C |
| • Internationalization and localization | iOS Apps, Topic 10-A |
| • App release | iOS Apps, Topic 10-B |
| **Domain 3.0 General Principles of Mobile Application Security** | |
| **Objective 3.1 Explain the need for mobile application security, and interpret security requirements and expectations** | |
| • Consequences of lax security | Android Apps, Topic 11-A<br>iOS Apps, Topic 9-C |
| • Information asset threats | iOS Apps, Topic 9-C |
| • Hacking | iOS Apps, Topic 9-C |
| • Untrusted networks | iOS Apps, Topic 9-C |
| • Development standards | Android Apps, Topics 2-A, 11-A, 11-B<br>iOS Apps, Topics 4-A, 9-C, 10-B |

| Exam Objective | Course, Lesson, and Topic Reference |
| --- | --- |
| • Platform requirements | Android Apps, Topics 2-A, 11-A, 11-B |
| | iOS Apps, Topics 4-A, 9-C, 10-B |
| • Google Play | Android Apps throughout |
| • Apple App Store | iOS Apps throughout |
| • Organizational processes and policies | Android Apps, Topic 11-A |
| • Least privilege | Android Apps, Topic 11-A |
| • Permissions | Android Apps, Topics 1-A, 2-A, 2-D, 3-B, 6-A, 7-B, 8-A, 10-B, 10-C, 11-A |
| | iOS Apps, Topics 8-A, 8-B, 9-C |

**Objective 3.2 Compare and contrast the Android and iOS security architectures**

| Exam Objective | Course, Lesson, and Topic Reference |
| --- | --- |
| • Platform strengths and weaknesses | Android Apps, Topics 1-A, 11-A |
| | iOS Apps, Topics 6-D, 9-C |
| • iOS architecture | iOS Apps, Topics 6-D, 9-C |
| • Layers | iOS Apps, Topic 1-B |
| • iOS security framework—hardware/firmware | iOS Apps, Topic 9-C |
| • iOS security framework—file system | iOS Apps, Topics 6-A, 9-C |
| • Android architecture | Android Apps, Topics 1-A, 11-A |
| • Linux kernel security | Android Apps, Topic 11-A |
| • Permission model | Android Apps, Topic 11-A |
| • Android/iOS vulnerabilities | Android Apps, Topics 1-A, 11-A |
| | iOS Apps, Topic 9-C |
| • Rooting/jailbreaking | iOS Apps, Topic 9-C |
| • Developer-caused | iOS Apps, Topic 9-C |
| • Third-party/unauthorized apps | iOS Apps, Topic 9-C |

**Objective 3.3 Implement mobile application development security measures**

| Exam Objective | Course, Lesson, and Topic Reference |
| --- | --- |
| • Security best practices | Android Apps, Topic 11-A |
| | iOS Apps, Topics 9-B, 9-C |
| • Authentication and authorization | iOS Apps, Topic 9-C |
| • Session management | iOS Apps, Topic 9-C |
| • Common threats | iOS Apps, Topics 9-B, 9-C |
| • SQL injection | iOS Apps, Topic 9-C |
| • Buffer overflows | iOS Apps, Topics 9-B, 9-C |
| • Input/output handling | Android Apps, Topics 6-A, 6-B |
| | iOS Apps, Topics 9-B, 9-C |

| Exam Objective | Course, Lesson, and Topic Reference |
| --- | --- |
| • Exceptions | Android Apps, Topics 7-A, 7-B<br>iOS Apps, Topics 9-A, 9-B |
| • Local device and process access | Android Apps, Topics 3-B, 11-A<br>iOS Apps, Topics 8-B, 9-C |
| • IPC | Android Apps, Topics 3-B, 11-A<br>iOS Apps, Topic 9-C |
| • Data encryption | Android Apps, Topics 11-A, 11-B<br>iOS Apps, Topics 2-A, 6-A, 9-C, 10-B |
| • Encryption approaches | Android Apps, Topic 11-A<br>iOS Apps, Topic 9-C |
| • Hashing | Android Apps, Topic 11-A |
| • JCA | Android Apps, Topic 11-A |
| • Crypto Engine certificates | iOS Apps, Topic 9-C |
| • Password salting | Android Apps, Topic 11-A |
| • Local storage access | Android Apps, Topics 6-A, 6-B, 11-A<br>iOS Apps, Topics 6-A, 8-B, 9-C |
| • Local storage types | Android Apps, Topics 6-A, 6-B<br>iOS Apps, Topics 6-A, 9-C |
| • File-based storage | Android Apps, Topics 6-A, 10-C, 11-B |
| • User preferences | Android Apps, Topics 9-A, 9-B<br>iOS Apps, Topic 9-C |
| • Keychain storage | iOS Apps, Topic 9-B |
| • SQLite databases | Android Apps, Topic 6-A<br>iOS Apps, Topic 9-B |
| • Directory structure | iOS Apps, Topic 6-A |
| • Threats to stored data | iOS Apps, Topics 6-A, 9-C |
| • Storage permissions | Android Apps, Topic 11-A<br>iOS Apps, Topics 8-B, 9-C |
| • Network and web communication security | Android Apps, Topic 11-A<br>iOS Apps, Topics 6-C, 9-C |
| • Input validation | Android Apps, Topic 11-A<br>iOS Apps, Topics 6-C, 9-C |
| • Secure network communication | iOS Apps, Topics 9-C |
| • WebView/UIWebView component use | Android Apps, Topic 8-B<br>iOS Apps, Topics 6-C, 9-C |
| • Java script injection | iOS Apps, Topic 9-C |

| Exam Objective | Course, Lesson, and Topic Reference |
|---|---|
| • Credential protection | iOS Apps, Topics 6-A, 9-C |
| • User authentication | iOS Apps, Topic 9-C |
| • App hardening techniques | Android Apps, Topics 7-B, 11-A, 11-B<br>iOS Apps, Topics 1-C, 9-A, 9-D |
| • Reverse/forward engineering | Android Apps, Topics 7-B, 11-B<br>iOS Apps, Topic 9-C |
| • Static/dynamic analysis | Android Apps, Topic 7-B<br>iOS Apps, Topic 9-A |
| • Data/code/stack trace obfuscation | Android Apps, Topic 11-B |
| • Password storage | Android Apps, Topic 11-A<br>iOS Apps, Topic 9-C |
| • Function naming | iOS Apps, Topic 1-D |

**Domain 4.0 Project Management Fundamentals**

**Objective 4.1 Identify basic project management concept**

| | |
|---|---|
| • Projects, programs, and portfolios | Project Management, Topic 1-B |
| • Stakeholders | Project Management, Topic 1-A |
| • Sponsors | Project Management, Topic 1-A |
| • Customers | Project Management, Topic 1-A |
| • Project managers | Project Management, Topic 1-A |
| • Team members | Project Management, Topic 1-A |
| • Deliverables | Project Management, Topic 1-B |
| • The project management process groups | Project Management, Topic 1-B |
| • Roles and responsibilities | Project Management, Topic 5-A |
| • Constraint factors | Project Management, Topic 2-A |
| • Time | Project Management, Topic 2-A |
| • Cost | Project Management, Topic 2-A |
| • Scope | Project Management, Topic 2-A |
| • Scope creep | Project Management, Topic 2-A |
| • Project objectives | Project Management, Topic 2-A |
| • Project assumptions | Project Management, Topic 2-A |
| • Risk | Project Management, Topics 2-C, 4-A, 4-B, 4-C |

**Objective 4.2 Define project requirements and create a project plan**

| | |
|---|---|
| • WBS | Project Management, Topic 3-A |

| Exam Objective | Course, Lesson, and Topic Reference |
| --- | --- |
| • Decomposition | Project Management, Topic 3-A |
| • Activities/sequencing | Project Management, Topic 3-B |
| • Dependencies | Project Management, Topic 3-B |
| • Precedence relationships | Project Management, Topic 3-B |
| • Resources | Project Management, Topic 3-C |
| • Estimation | Project Management, Topic 3-C |
| • Leveling | Project Management, Topic 3-C |
| • The critical path | Project Management, Topic 3-C |
| • Float | Project Management, Topic 3-C |
| • Baselines | Project Management, Topic 3-C |
| • Costs | Project Management, Topic 3-D |
| • Estimates | Project Management, Topic 3-D |
| • Budgeting | Project Management, Topic 3-D |
| • Cost baselines | Project Management, Topic 3-D |
| • Risk analysis | Project Management, Topic 4-A |
| • Communication plans | Project Management, Topic 4-B |
| • Change control | Project Management, Topic 4-C |
| **Objective 4.3 Execute an app development plan** | |
| • Project work | Project Management, Topic 4-A |
| • Quality assurance | Project Management, Topic 4-B |
| • Tracking project progress | Project Management, Topic 4-C |
| • EVA | Project Management, Topic 4-C |
| • Variance | Project Management, Topic 4-C |
| • Performance reporting | Project Management, Topic 4-D |
| • Project closeout | Project Management, Topics 6-A, 6-B |
| • Closeout elements | Project Management, Topic 6-A |
| • Final reports | Project Management, Topic 6-B |

# Solutions

## ACTIVITY 1–1: Identifying Project Basics

1. What are the characteristics of the project that Rita's team is working on that make it a project instead of an operational task?

   A: Answers may include a definite end date, tasks that do not repeat, or a one-time deliverable.

2. Who are the stakeholders (project manager, customer, sponsor, project team, project management team) for the training manual project?

   A: The project manager is Rita, the customer is the tax return processing team, the sponsor is Bob, the project team is the team members that report to Rita, and the project management team includes you and Rita.

3. It is common for project teams to have part-time members who also perform operational tasks. Which team members also have operational tasks? What are the operational tasks? How might this impact the project?

   A: Answers will vary, but an example is that the tax return processors must still perform their regular job, their operational tasks include processing the tax returns, and this could impact the project as they may not always be available to work on project tasks.

## ACTIVITY 1–2: Identifying the Project Management Life Cycle

1. Which definition best describes project management?

   ○   Management of a collection of programs to ensure that all projects in the collection contribute to achieving the organization's strategic goals.

   ◉   Management of project activities to meet project objectives through the application of knowledge, skills, tools, and techniques to those activities.

   ○   Management of a collection of projects in a centralized and coordinated manner to achieve collective objectives and benefits.

   ○   Management of day-to-day activities to sustain the business.

2. Give some examples of a portfolio and the programs and projects of which it is made up.

   A: Answers will vary, but should be hierarchical. For example, a software company may have a game portfolio that contains a program for each of its titles and projects to develop new versions within those programs.

3. **Which of these is the name of a project management process group?**
   ○ Verification
   ○ Prototyping
   ◉ Planning
   ○ Designing

4. **True or False? A project deliverable requires the approval and sign-off of project stakeholders.**
   ☑ True
   ☐ False

5. **Which project management process group allows you to identify problems and take corrective action?**
   ◉ Monitoring and Controlling
   ○ Execution
   ○ Planning
   ○ Initiation

6. **In which project management process group will you define a project's objectives and organize for the course of action to be taken?**
   ○ Initiation
   ○ Execution
   ○ Monitoring and Controlling
   ◉ Planning

---

# ACTIVITY 1–3: Identifying the Role of a Project Manager

---

1. **What skills do you require to ensure that the team is not bogged down by the market expectations and the celebrity of Steve Jones? (Choose two.)**
   ☐ Culinary skills
   ☑ Good communication and negotiation skills
   ☑ Ability to motivate the team
   ☐ Complete project management knowledge

2. **As a software project, what IT project considerations might complicate the progress?**

   **A:** Answers might include: an intangible deliverable, conflict between expectations and developer's design, dependencies on related software or infrastructure projects.

3. **The development team involves resources who perform different functions. Which organizational structure will give you the greatest control over the entire team?**
   ○ Composite
   ○ Functional
   ○ Matrix
   ◉ Projectized

4. Steve Jones's TV schedule may frequently interfere with your project's schedules and affect the working hours of the other resources. What roles do you need to play to resolve this problem? (Choose two.)

   ☑ Manage the overall schedule of the project so that Jones's TV schedules do not hamper the successful completion of the project.

   ☐ Proactively communicate project information to the project team and the stakeholders.

   ☑ Coordinate resources and motivate them to work toward the success of the project, in spite of the issues about the availability of the chef.

   ☐ Identify the impact of the project on the organization's strategic plans.

# ACTIVITY 2–1: Examining a Project Scope Statement

3. Which of the following are out of scope for the project? (Choose two.)

   ☑ The actual transportation of the fireworks.

   ☐ A detailed report of the recommended route and modes of transportation.

   ☑ Negotiation of reduced costs with potential logistics companies.

   ☐ An appendix containing the details of the research and calculations.

4. Which is a constraint to the project?

   ○ Contract approval

   ◉ Modes of recommended transport must allow fireworks

   ○ Cost of transport

   ○ Page limit set for the report

5. True or False? Things that limit the handling of a project are called constraints?

   ☑ True

   ☐ False

6. True or False? Objectives of a project need not necessarily be measurable.

   ☐ True

   ☑ False

7. Which of the following should be captured while examining the scope of the project? (Choose three.)

   ☑ Project assumptions

   ☐ The ways in which the project team will accomplish its objectives

   ☑ The benefits that the project will have for the organization

   ☑ Project constraints

# ACTIVITY 2–2: Identifying Skills Using the Skills Matrix

1. If you were the project manager for the project, how would you respond to the blank spaces?

   **A:** Answers will vary, but should include the options of adding team members with the missing skills or providing training for team members.

2. **The video director, Jen Baker, is not in a position to continue in the team due to unavoidable circumstances. The management is now contemplating the right person to take her position and complete the tasks. Who do you think might be the right person to replace Jen Baker?**

   A: Answers will vary, but should include the possibility of Tom Wu, depending on his experience and the amount of video left to produce.

3. **True or False? Based on the empty spaces in the matrix, you need to hire an audio producer and developers.**
   - ☑ True
   - ☐ False

4. **Which team member would be most difficult to replace?**
   - ○ Tom Wu
   - ◉ Steve Jones
   - ○ Maria Ruiz
   - ○ Jen Baker

5. **What are the uses of a team skills matrix? (Choose three.)**
   - ☐ Identify the availability of team members.
   - ☑ Identify which team members have the required skillsets.
   - ☑ Break out skills needed for each project task.
   - ☑ Identify criteria that may be used to determine whether a team member has a particular skillset.

# ACTIVITY 2–3: Identifying Sources of Risk

1. **Spend a few minutes brainstorming with your group some of the obvious project risks. Make sure to record these for use in later activities.**

   A: Answers will vary, but may include the celebrity chef's schedule, hiring resources, technology concerns, and so on.

2. **There may be risks that you have not yet identified. Use the following risk category list to prompt your group to think of more risks and add them to your list: Budget/funding, Schedule, Changes to scope/requirements, Technical issues, Personnel issues, Hardware, Contracts, and Political/legal concerns.**

   A: Answers will vary, but may include withdrawal of funding by the television network, schedule changes due to availability of Steve Jones, addition of new features to the game, issues with the software development platform, personality conflicts between the team members, backorder of computer equipment for developers, contractual conflicts, and risk of offensive material.

# ACTIVITY 3–1: Creating a Work Breakdown Structure

1. **Working with your group, create a list of the work packages that make up this deliverable.**

   A: Answers will vary, but may include technical requirements document, storyboard, and screenshots.

2. Spend a few minutes decomposing a few of the items you listed as work packages. Write out some of the tasks that may be needed to complete the items. Be sure to consider tasks that need to happen before deliverable work can begin, such as research, purchasing hardware, interviews, and so on.

   **A:** Answers will vary, but may include interviewing Steve Jones for vision, asset research, tools availability research, create storyboard, write sample dialog, and so on.

# ACTIVITY 3-2: Sequencing Activities in a Project Schedule Network Diagram

3. According to the project schedule network diagram, which is the "Create animation" task's predecessor activity?
   - ○ Edit sequence
   - ○ Create subtitles
   - ◉ Record audio
   - ○ Write dialog

4. What task can be done in parallel with the "Record audio" task?
   - ○ Write dialog
   - ○ Edit sequence
   - ◉ Create subtitles
   - ○ None

# ACTIVITY 3-3: Creating a Project Schedule

1. In the given project schedule, the ES value of Task 1 is 0 and duration is 5. What will be the calculated EF value of Task 1? Fill in the ES and EF values in the diagram provided for all the steps in this activity.

   **A:** The early finish of Task 1 = Duration of Task 1. Therefore, the EF value of Task 1 is 5.

2. What will be the early start value of Task 2?

   **A:** The early start of Task 2 = The early finish of Task 1. Therefore, the ES value of Task 2 is 5.

3. Calculate the early finish value of Task 2, given the early start value is 5 and duration is 4.

   **A:** The early finish of Task 2 = The early finish of Task 1 + Duration of Task 2. Therefore, the EF value of Task 2 is 9.

4. Consider the early finish value of Task 2 as 9, the duration of Task 3 as 6, and the duration of Task 4 as 10. What will be the early start and early finish values of Tasks 3 and 4?

   **A:** The early start of Tasks 3 and 4 = The early finish of Task 2. Therefore, the early start of Tasks 3 and 4 is 9. The early finish of Task 3 = The early start of Task 3 + Duration of Task 3 and the early finish of Task 4 = The early start of Task 4 + Duration of Task 4. Therefore, the early finish of Tasks 3 and 4 are 15 and 19.

5. What will be the early start and early finish values for Task 5?

   **A:** The early start of Task 5 = Maximum early finish values of Tasks 3 and 4. The early finish of Task 5 = The early start of Task 5 + Duration of Task 5. Therefore, the early start and early finish values of Task 5 are 19 and 24.

6. **What are the early start and early finish values of Tasks 6, 7, 8, and 9?**

   **A:** The early start and early finish values of Tasks 6, 7, 8, and 9 can be calculated as before. The early start values of Tasks 6, 7, 8, and 9 are 24, 24, 24, and 34. The early finish values of Tasks 6, 7, 8, and 9 are 34, 34, 32, and 54.

7. **For Task 9, the early start value is 34 and early finish value is 54. What will be the calculated late finish value of Task 9?**

   **A:** The late finish of Task 9 = The early finish of Task 9. Therefore, the LF of Task 9 is 54.

8. **The late finish value of Task 9 is 54. What is the late start value of Task 9?**

   **A:** The late start value of Task 9 = The late finish value of Task 9 – Duration of Task 9. Therefore, the LS value of Task 9 is 34.

9. **What are the late finish and late start values of Task 8?**

   **A:** The late finish of Task 8 = The late start of Task 9 and the late start of Task 8 = The late finish of Task 8 – Duration of Task 8.

10. **What are the late finish and late start values for Tasks 6 and 7?**

    **A:** Calculating the LF and LS values is similar to the earlier steps. The late start for Tasks 6 and 7 is 24. The late finish for Tasks 6 and 7 is 34.

11. **What are the late finish and late start values for Task 5?**

    **A:** The late finish of Task 5 = Minimum late start values of Tasks 6, 7, and 8. The late start of Task 5 = The late finish of Task 5 – Duration of Task 5.

12. **What are the late finish and late start values for Tasks 1, 2, 3, and 4?**

    **A:** For Task 1, LF = 5 and LS = 0; Task 2, LF = 9 and LS = 5; Task 3, LF = 19 and LS = 13; Task 4, LF = 19 and LS = 9.

13. **Which is a valid critical path for this project?**

    - ○ 1, 2, 4, 5, 8, 9
    - ○ 1, 2, 3, 5, 6, 9
    - ◉ 1, 2, 4, 5, 6, 9
    - ○ 1, 2, 3, 5, 8, 9

14. **What is the duration of the critical path?**

    - ◉ 54
    - ○ 56
    - ○ 52
    - ○ 50

15. **Which activities in the project do not fall on the critical path? (Choose two.)**

    - ☐ Task 6
    - ☐ Task 4
    - ☑ Task 3
    - ☑ Task 8

# ACTIVITY 3-4: Determining Project Costs

1. What information does the cost estimate of an activity in the project convey?
   - ○ The cost incurred by the activity in a similar past project.
   - ◉ The planned cost of resources required to perform the activity.
   - ○ The project's budgeted cost.
   - ○ The pay received by each resource per hour.

2. True or False? During the cost budgeting of the cooking reality show game application project, you need to take Steve Jones's contract information into account.
   - ☑ True
   - ☐ False

3. Upon cost budgeting the game application project, what important analyses can the stakeholders perform? (Choose two.)
   - ☑ Assess the financial feasibility of the project.
   - ☐ Determine market demand for the application.
   - ☑ Determine additional funding requirements.
   - ☐ Identify the risks to the project.

# ACTIVITY 4-1: Analyzing the Risks to a Project

1. Using the provided Risk Probability and Impact Assessment chart, work with your group to fill in some of the project risks and estimate their probability and impact on a scale of 1 to 5 (5 is very high, 1 is very low).

   **A:** Answers will vary, but may include personality conflicts, technical issues, and so on.

2. In the Risk Probability and Impact Assessment table, fill in the Risk Score for each risk by multiplying the probability by the impact.

   **A:** Answers will vary depending on student responses.

3. Which of your risks has the highest Risk Score? What is a possible risk response plan?

   **A:** Answers will vary depending on student responses, but may include hiring a voice actor that can imitate Steve Jones, replacing videos with stills where necessary, and so on.

# ACTIVITY 4-2: Creating a Communication Management Plan

2. On the second line of the communications plan, fill in the Medium and Owner columns. Keep in mind that the team is not working in one place.

   **A:** Answers will vary, but may include Conference Call as Medium and Project Manager as Owner

3. Who is the audience for the Monthly Status Meetings? Fill in the Audience column for the Monthly Status Meeting row.

   **A:** Answers will vary, but may include Project Team and Stakeholders.

4.  In the first empty row, enter the information for the Visual Design Team Meetings. Use the Technical Design Meetings row as a guideline.

    **A:** Answers will vary, but should include Visual Design Meetings, and the Visual Design lead as owner.

5.  In the last empty row, enter the information for the Daily Leads Meetings.

    **A:** Answers will vary, but should include "Daily" in the Frequency column, and "Project Leads" in the Audience column.

# ACTIVITY 4-3: Developing a Change Control Plan

1.  Who will you involve in the change control planning for the project?
    - ○ Steve Jones
    - ◉ Key stakeholders
    - ○ Team members
    - ○ Implementation team members

2.  True or False? Only team members are authorized to initiate a change request.
    - ☐ True
    - ☑ False

3.  Who would make the decision about whether or not a change is necessary?
    - ○ Stakeholders
    - ◉ Stakeholders and the project team
    - ○ Core team members
    - ○ The project team

4.  True or False? Changes in a project do not usually affect the quality of the project.
    - ☐ True
    - ☑ False

# ACTIVITY 5-1: Beginning Project Work

1.  Identify the project manager. The project manager introduces the key players in the project.

    **A:** The student who volunteers as project manager should introduce the other classmates and their roles.

2.  The project manager asks the project sponsor to give an overview of the project objectives.

    **A:** The student acting as project manager will ask the instructor to give an overview and then the instructor will do so.

3.  The project manager asks the team to ask questions and allows anyone to answer as appropriate.

    **A:** The student who volunteers as project manager should take questions and either answer or direct to appropriate players.

# ACTIVITY 5–2: Executing the Project Plan

1. True or False? The team should work on whatever tasks they want to regardless of the project plan.
   - ☐ True
   - ☑ False

2. True or False? Conducting weekly team meetings helps in ensuring that the project schedule completion dates are met.
   - ☑ True
   - ☐ False

3. Your team needs to design and develop a game that is fun and represents the Steve Jones show. What should you do to help them meet their objectives?
   - ○ Command them to come to work on time.
   - ○ Teach them to cook.
   - ◉ Monitor their general work performance and keep an eye on how well they adhere to company policies.
   - ○ Make sure they design it the way you would do it.

# ACTIVITY 5–3: Calculating Earned Value

1. What is the earned value for this work package?
   - ○ $7,500
   - ○ $5,000
   - ◉ $3,000
   - ○ $2,500

2. Calculate planned value for the "Develop Storyboard" work package for the actual number of days.
   - ○ $2,500
   - ○ $500
   - ○ $4,500
   - ◉ $5,000

3. What is the cost variance for the work package?
   - ○ $3,000
   - ○ $2,500
   - ○ $1,000
   - ◉ $500

4. What does the cost variance indicate?
   - ○ The project is over budget by $500.
   - ◉ The project is under budget by $500.
   - ○ The project is over budget by $2,500.
   - ○ The project is under budget by $2,500.

5. **What formula would you use to calculate SPI?**
   - ○ EV – PV
   - ◉ EV / PV
   - ○ EV – AC
   - ○ EV / AC

6. **Calculate the CPI for the project.**
   - ○ 1.4
   - ○ 0.1
   - ◉ 1.2
   - ○ 0.2

7. **What does the Cost Performance Index (CPI) of 1.2 for the project indicate?**
   - ◉ The project is performing under budget.
   - ○ The project is performing over budget.
   - ○ The project is within budget.
   - ○ The project is behind schedule and is over budget.

8. **True or False? SPI of 1.0 means the project is right on schedule.**
   - ☑ True
   - ☐ False

9. **Identify a benefit of conducting the earned value analysis.**
   - ○ It provides a more accurate project baseline than other tracking methods.
   - ◉ It allows you to track project performance and also acts as a means to forecast project performance.
   - ○ Management can understand earned value analysis better than other measures.
   - ○ Helps identify what the project team has accomplished so far.

10. **Your team has been working well ever since the project started. But, over the past couple of weeks, you have observed a dip in performance. What steps can you take to help the team perform better? (Choose two.)**
    - ☐ During team meetings, shower praise on members who performed well and condemn the non-performers.
    - ☐ Tighten the deadlines to improve productivity.
    - ☑ Encourage team members to share their experiences with others.
    - ☑ Appreciate good efforts during team meetings and organize events for recognizing team members who have performed well.

---

# ACTIVITY 5–4: Reporting Project Performance

---

1. **What information does a status report convey to the stakeholders?**
   - ○ The exemplary performance of one of the assistant chefs.
   - ○ A prediction of the final cost the project will incur.
   - ◉ A description of the project costs and schedules for the current reporting period.
   - ○ The conflicts between the team members and how the project manager resolved them.

2. **What is a benefit of a project forecast report to the project team and the senior management?**
   - ○ Pinpoints the problem areas of the project.
   - ◉ Identifies where the project will stand if it progresses at the current rate.
   - ○ Identifies the team members responsible for the projected success or failure of the project.
   - ○ Analyzes the status of the project as against original plans.

3. **True or False? Personnel evaluations help to identify the training requirements of a project team.**
   - ☑ True
   - ☐ False

# ACTIVITY 5–5: Implementing Change Control

2. **Based on the information in the change request, what action should you take? (Choose two.)**
   - ☐ Bring information to all the team members for evaluation.
   - ☐ Coordinate changes across knowledge areas.
   - ☑ Identify corrective action to be taken to resolve the problem.
   - ☑ Bring information to all the key stakeholders.
   - ☐ Update the project plan to reflect changes.

3. **Who will you involve in the change control process for the project?**
   - ○ People involved in the project.
   - ○ All the team members.
   - ◉ Key stakeholders.
   - ○ Implementation team members.

4. **True or False? Change requests should be justified before analysis.**
   - ☑ True
   - ☐ False

# ACTIVITY 6–1: Closing a Project

1. **What is an element of project closeout that requires the stakeholders' acceptance?**
   - ○ Recipes included in the application.
   - ○ Minutes of all project status meetings.
   - ◉ The final code and installation packages of the game.
   - ○ Documentation of lessons learned from the project.

2. **What project information is important and needs to be archived for future reference? (Choose two.)**
   - ☐ Audio and video shooting activities for the animations.
   - ☑ The deviations in the project schedules, reasons for the deviations, and steps taken to keep the project on track.
   - ☐ Steve Jones's autograph and photographs with the project team.
   - ☑ Variances between planned cost and actual cost, and steps taken to keep the project as much within budget as possible.

3. True or False? You need to bring Steve Jones's contract agreement to a formal closure as part of the project closeout process.

   ☑ True

   ☐ False

4. What activity will you perform as part of the project closeout process?

   ○ Collect anecdotes from Steve Jones.

   ◉ Obtain a formal acceptance of the project deliverables from the stakeholders.

   ○ Shoot pictures of the food cooked while creating video animations.

   ○ Bring major project issues to the notice of the senior management.

---

# ACTIVITY 6-2: Creating a Final Report

---

1. What information would you include in the final report of the project? (Choose two.)

   ☐ A list of files and documentation generated during the project's life cycle.

   ☐ Documentation of the contract signed with Steve Jones.

   ☑ The outstanding coordination within the project team that ensured completion of the project on time and within budget.

   ☑ Steve Jones was unable to complete the final audio recording and the audio engineer had to recreate some pieces from pre-recorded words.

2. True or False? The final report is presented to the stakeholders, the project team, and the senior management.

   ☑ True

   ☐ False

3. One of the developers was a wonderful worker. She always showed up prepared, worked hard and smart, and was willing to do more than her share of project tasks. However, she skipped or was late for at least 50 percent of the team meetings. What commentary would you include while evaluating her performance in the final report? (Choose three.)

   ☑ The developer's unwillingness to participate in team meetings made things more difficult for others on the team.

   ☑ She made group decision making harder.

   ☑ She made team communication more complex, and her absence was probably a morale buster.

   ☐ Though she was unwilling to attend the meetings, her work compensated for her behavior.

4. What is a valid recommendation for future projects?

   ○ Hire Steve Jones as the key personality for all future game projects.

   ○ Strive to complete projects ahead of scheduled time by stretching the working time of resources.

   ◉ Establish a communication protocol among the project team and stakeholders.

   ○ Compensate on the quality of the product if the cost to the company can be reduced.

# Glossary

**AC**
(Actual Cost) The total cost incurred in accomplishing a task within a period of time.

**activity**
A unit of project work that must be performed to complete a project deliverable.

**activity dependency**
A logical relationship between two activities that indicates whether the start of an activity depends upon an event or input from another activity or an external factor.

**activity sequencing**
The task of identifying and documenting the relationships among the activities, and arranging the activities in a sequence based on those relationships.

**BAC**
(Budget At Completion) The total sum of the budget for a project.

**change control**
The process of identifying, documenting, approving or rejecting, and controlling changes to the project baselines.

**communication plan**
A plan which describes what information must be communicated to whom, by whom, when, and in what manner.

**cost baseline**
A summation of the estimated costs of the activities by period, which serves as the basis for measuring the project's performance against budget.

**cost budgeting**
The process of aggregating the cost estimates of all the activities or work packages to arrive at an overall cost estimate for the project.

**cost estimate**
An assessment of the likely costs of resources required to complete an activity.

**CPI**
(Cost Performance Index) A measurement of cost efficiency, calculated by dividing EV by AC.

**critical path**
The path in the project schedule network diagram that has the longest duration.

**CV**
(Cost Variance) The difference between the earned value and the actual cost incurred, calculated by subtracting AC from EV.

**decomposition**
A technique for creating the WBS by subdividing project deliverables to the work package level.

### duration estimation
The act of estimating the period required to complete the project activities.

### EAC
(Estimate At Completion) The projected final costs of work when the project is completed, calculated by adding ETC and AC.

### earned value analysis
A method of analyzing the project progress by comparing actual schedule and cost performance against planned performance as laid out in the cost and schedule baseline.

### ETC
(Estimate To Complete) An estimate of how much more cost is to be incurred to complete the project, calculated by subtracting EV from BAC and optionally dividing the result by CPI to adjust according to current variance trend.

### EV
(Earned Value) The value of work actually accomplished, calculated by multiplying the percentage of work completed by the BAC.

### final report
A report that summarizes what happened in the project.

### float
The amount of time an activity can be delayed without delaying the ES of the immediate successor activity.

### kick–off meeting
A meeting conducted by the project manager at the beginning of the project wherein stakeholders share the importance, objectives, and intended scope of the project.

### lag
A modification in a logical relationship that delays the start of a successor activity.

### lead
A modification in a logical relationship that allows the successor activity to start before the predecessor activity ends.

### performance reporting
The process of gathering and communicating information regarding the current status of a project as well as projections for progress over time.

### portfolio
A collection of programs that are grouped together to achieve an organization's strategic business objectives.

### portfolio management
Management of a portfolio to ensure that all projects in the portfolio contribute to achieving the organization's strategic goals.

### precedence relationship
A logical relationship between two activities that indicates which activity should be performed first and which one should be performed later.

### program
A group of related and interrelated projects that have a common objective.

### program management
Management of a program in a centralized and coordinated manner to achieve a set of strategic objectives.

### project
A temporary endeavor that creates a unique product, service, or result.

### project assumptions
Statements that must be taken to be true in order for the project planning to begin.

### project charter
A document that provides a clear and concise description of the business needs that the project is intended to address.

### project closeout
Process of closing out all project activities and formally ending the project or, in the

case of multiphase projects, closing out a specific project phase.

## project deliverable
An output from a project management activity that is measurable, unique, and verifiable.

## project life cycle
The sequential phases of work done on a project, including all planning, work activities, and closure; it is marked by the beginning and the end of the project.

## project management
The management of project activities to meet project objectives through the application of knowledge, skills, tools, and techniques to those activities.

## Project Management Office
An administrative unit that supervises and coordinates the management of all projects in an organization.

## project objectives
The criteria used to measure whether a project is successful or not.

## project phases
A group of related project activities that result in the completion of a major deliverable.

## project schedule network diagram
A graphical representation of the activities in a project and the logical relationships between those activities.

## project stakeholder
A person who has a business interest in the outcome of a project.

## project team
A group of individuals who collectively have the skills required to complete a project.

## PV
(Planned Value) The budgeted cost to be spent on a task within a period of time.

## QA
(quality assurance) A method of evaluating overall project performance through planned, systematic activities; it creates confidence that the project will adhere to the appropriate processes and satisfy standards for quality.

## qualitative analysis
A method of assessing, ranking, and prioritizing risks for subsequent analysis, taking into account the probability of different risks occurring and their likely impact.

## quantitative analysis
A numerical method used to assess the impact of risk and to measure the amount of damage that can take place, which further refines and enhances the prioritization and scoring produced during qualitative analysis.

## resource estimation
The means of determining the resources required to complete project activities.

## resources
The people, equipment, materials, or other costs that are used to accomplish a project task.

## risk
An uncertain event that may have a positive or a negative effect on a project.

## risk response plan
A plan used to decrease the possibility or impact of risk in order to accomplish project objectives.

## schedule baseline
A snapshot of the schedule before the project begins execution, which is approved by stakeholders and serves as the basis for measuring project progress.

## scope creep
The additional task items that are added to a project as the project progresses and make it difficult to achieve project goals.

## scope definition process
The process of documenting the project's parameters, its objectives, requirements, and deliverables in the project scope statement.

## scope statement
An itemized definition of the agreed upon outcome of a project.

### SOW

(Statement of Work) A document that describes the products or services that a project will supply. It specifies the work that will be done during the project and defines the business need that it is designed to meet.

### SPI

(Schedule Performance Index) The ratio of work performed to work scheduled, calculated by dividing EV by PV.

### SV

(Schedule Variance) The difference between the work actually performed and the work scheduled, calculated by subtracting PV from EV.

### team skills matrix

A table listing the skills required to complete the project, which assists in selecting team members and identifying gaps.

### total float

The amount of time an activity can be delayed from its ES without delaying the project finish date.

### VAC

(Variance At Completion) The difference between EAC and BAC.

### WBS

(work breakdown structure) A hierarchical structure that subdivides project deliverables and project work into smaller, more manageable pieces of work.

# Index


**A**

AC *72*
activity
    defined *39*
    dependency *39*
    sequencing *39*
Actual Cost, *See* AC

**B**

BAC *72*
Budget At Completion, *See* BAC

**C**

change
    control *60*
    requests *80*
communication plans *57*
constraining factors *19*
cost
    baselines *49*
    budgeting *49*
    estimates *49*
Cost Performance Index, *See* CPI
Cost Variance, *See* CV
CPI *73*
critical paths *45*
CV *73*

**D**

decomposition *36*
dependencies *39*
duration estimations *44*

**E**

EAC *73*
Earned Value, *See* EV
earned value analysis *72*
earned value calculations *72*
Estimate At Completion, *See* EAC
Estimate To Complete, *See* ETC
ETC *73*
EV *72*

**F**

final reports *86*
float
    definition of *45*
    total float *45*

**I**

IT projects *11*

**K**

kick-off meetings *66*

**L**

lag *41*
lead *41*

**O**

operational tasks *2*
organizational structures *11*

**P**

performance indices *73*
performance reporting *77*
performance reports
    type of *77*
Planned Value, *See* PV
PMO *11*
portfolio
    defined *6*
    management *7*
precedence relationships *40*
program
    defined *5*
    management *6*
project
    assumptions *19*
    charters *21*
    closeout *84*
    defined *2*
    deliverables *7*
    execution process *69*
    life cycle *2*
    management *5*
    management life cycle *8*
    management process groups *8*
    management software *12*
    manager roles *12*
    managers *10*
    need for *3*
    objectives *20*
    phases *2*
    resources *43*
    schedule network diagrams *40*
    stakeholders *3*
Project Management Office, *See* PMO
project teams
    defined *24*
    members of *24*
    virtual *24*
PV *72*

**Q**

qualitative analysis *54*
quality assurance *69*
quantitative analysis *54*

**R**

resource
    estimations *43*
    leveling *43*
resources
    defined *43*
risk
    identifying *30*
    response plans *54*
risks *29*

**S**

schedule
    baselines *46*
    development terms *44*
Schedule Performance Index, *See* SPI
Schedule Variance, *See* SV
scope
    creep *18*
    definition process *20*
    statements *18*
    statements, creating *22*
SOW *21*
SPI *73*
Statement of Work, *See* SOW
SV *73*

**T**

team acquisition process *66*
team skills matrix *25*
total float *45*

**V**

VAC *73*
variance
    identification *72*
    management *73*
Variance At Completion, *See* VAC
virtual project teams *24*

**W**

WBS *36*
work breakdown structure, *See* WBS